tapas
a bite of SPAIN

Janet Mendel

PHOTOGRAPHY BY MICHELLE CHAPLOW

TAPAS – A BITE OF SPAIN

Published by Ediciones Santana, S.L.
Apartado 41
29650 Mijas-Pueblo (Málaga)
Spain

Tel: (0034) 952 48 58 38
E-Mail: info@santanabooks.com
www.santanabooks.com

Text Copyright © 2008 Janet Mendel

Photography Copyright © 2008 Michelle Chaplow

Designed by Cheryl Gatward of Newimage

Printed in Spain by Industrias Gráficas Solprint, S.L.

ISBN: 978-84-89954-77-9
Depósito Legal: MA-1.903/2008

ACKNOWLEDGEMENTS

Many thanks to Donna Ellefson, for her help with editing and shaping this book, and to Gertrud Roberts of Santana Books for the final editing.

Thanks to tapa bar cooks everywhere in Spain who contributed their recipes and hints. Thanks to the following who also helped me on the tapas trail: John Davies, Amanda Clark, Carlos Pilkington and Benjamin Searl. Thanks to Michelle Chaplow and her team for the great pictures in this book and special thanks to photographer Dominique Dallet for coming through with an author photo.

I am especially grateful to Cheryl Gatward for design and layout. She has made this book appealing to look at and easy to use in the kitchen.

Michelle Chaplow would like to thank her assistant photographers and food stylists David Doyle and Joaquin Alarcón.

Very special thanks also to Issac Mariscal, Noella López and Chef Francisco Adame of La Menorah en Finca Cortesìn for allowing us to shoot overnight in their restaurant.

Location sites
El Espejo, Madrid
Costa Gallega, Barcelona
Sagardi Euskal Taberna, Barcelona
Bar Faustino, Ronda
Tragatapas, Ronda
Baranka Resturant, San Sebastian
La Bodega de la Alfalfa, Sevilla
Sol y Sombra Sevilla, Sevilla
Bar Juanitos, Jerez
La Vicaria, Arcos de la Frontera

FOREWORD

I love tapas—a variety of tastes, enjoyed with wine and with friends. For me, they are the essence of life in Spain. This is both a cookbook and a guidebook. It starts with a tasting guide to tapas round Spain—how to enjoy them and what to eat. Then I show you how to translate those great dishes to your own kitchen.

I've selected my favourite tapas, the ones that I enjoy cooking and serving to friends. They are based on traditional Spanish products. Recipes are chosen and tested for the home kitchen. You don't have to go to chef's school in order to prepare them.

I have not included recipes for tapas that are especially labour-intensive, such as the famous *callos a la madrileña*, Madrid-style tripe in a piquant sauce. Let the cook in a tapa bar prepare a whole calf's hock and tripe! (If you really want the recipe for tripe stew or snails or *cocido*, a one-pot dinner, please consult *Cooking in Spain*, my definitive guide to Spanish cooking.)

The recipes are arranged by the way tapas are prepared and served— spread on toast, stuck on a cocktail stick, in a cold salad, hot off the griddle, in a cooked dish with sauce —rather than by food category (eggs, seafood, meat). Thus, prawns, for example, could well appear in every single chapter. If you're looking for a great way to cook a particular food, whether it be prawns, artichokes, clams or sausage, please consult the Index to find recipes with that ingredient.

Many tapas can be turned into starters or main dishes by increasing the serving size and adding accompaniments. I'll give you suggestions in recipes throughout the book. You'll find menu ideas in Planning a Tapas Party.

Many sauces and dressings, such as *alioli*, garlic mayonnaise, and *romesco*, red pepper and nut sauce, are called for in different recipes throughout the book. So I have grouped them all together in one chapter. Individual recipes will give you a page reference. But, feel free to ad-lib—you may love that romesco so much you want it with steak, or the Cabrales blue-cheese sauce as a dip with endive leaves.

If you find Spanish words that puzzle you please look at the Glossary on page 280. (For example, what's *cava*? Cava is Spanish bubbly, made by the *méthode champenoise*).

Measurements for ingredients are given in three standards, metric, British and American, in that order. Tablespoons and teaspoons are always level measures. Where British and American terminology differs, the British is given first and the American follows in parentheses. For example: aubergine (eggplant) and grill (broiler).

Most recipes specify simply "olive oil." While extra virgin oil is preferred, you can use plain olive oil. Where extra virgin oil is essential, it is called for specifically.

¡Qué aproveche! I hope you enjoy tapas, in Spain and in your own home.

Janet Mendel

CONTENTS

THE TAPAS WAY OF LIFE

THE TAPAS WAY OF LIFE

Here, take a taste. An olive. A slice of salt-cured ham. A sweet, briny prawn. Sip a little fino Sherry. Laugh and savour the moment. Pure essence of Spain, that's what tapas are. A way of life.

Tapas are small bites of food served with wine. They are a very old custom in Spain. So old, in fact, that no one quite knows how it all started. The custom originated in the wine-growing regions of Andalusia, such as Jerez, where Sherry comes from. Tapas probably began in the *bodegas*, where wine is dispensed from barrels, and in the taverns where the wine is drunk.

The word *tapa* means a cover or lid. Why put a lid on the wine? Fermented grape juice attracts tiny fruit flies. To prevent their swarming into a glass of wine, the bar-keep would cover the wine with a tiny saucer.

Once the little saucer was set on the wine glass, it was an obvious next step to place a few olives or a slice of the house-made sausage on the dish. The tavern with the best selection of "lids," tapas, would draw more customers.

Or, you could opt for another explanation for tapas—the royal edict. Back in 1264, King Alfonso X "The Wise" wrote a treatise on Sherry and stipulated that imbibers of wine take small bites of food, to temper the effects of the alcohol.

In any case, tapas and Sherry create a perfect symbiosis, for bites of food make it possible to keep sipping the wine. Sherry and the other fortified aperitif wines of Andalusia, with between 15.5 and 20 percent alcohol (most table wines have between 11 and 13 percent alcohol), require food to aid in the assimilation of the alcohol. You eat in order to better drink.

So intimately related are tapas with wine that, in many Andalusian bars, it once was customary to serve a tapa free with every glass of wine. The tapa was, perhaps, nothing more than a few olives or a single golden croquette, but, nevertheless, the custom became established. Rivalry and competition led to more and better tapas.

As the custom has evolved, however, the complimentary tapa has tended to disappear. Instead, customers order from a list of tapas and pay for them accordingly. In some bars, the list is chalked on a board; in others the waiter spiels off in rapid-fire the *pregón*, or selection. You might catch a few of the dozens he recites. Some waiters are *monstruos*, "monsters"—cheeky, in-your-face, but superb at keeping the glasses filled and the plates of food coming. If you don't catch the recitation, press your way up to the bar and have a look at the platters of food on display. Some bars change the list every few days. In others, you can count on the same old favourites forever. Spain is known for its late, late dining hours (between 2 and 3 pm for the main, midday meal and 9 and10 pm for the evening meal). In this culture, a preprandial bite to eat becomes a matter of sustenance.

A tapa is a small, individual portion, really just a bite or two. Tapa etiquette varies from one region to another. In Andalusian towns, you might be served a free tapa with your glass of wine, but then be shown a list of

specialties offered in three sizes (and three prices)—tapa, *media ración* (half plate) and *ración* (whole plate). Occasionally, the barman adds up the bill by counting the number of plates you have accumulated.

In Madrid bars, you order by *ración*. Your bill might be chalked right on the bar. In the Basque Country, you can serve yourself from a line-up of pintxos, all stuck with cocktail sticks. Keep those sticks, because the barman will add them up to calculate your bill.

In Spain, it's part of the tapas way of life to stop in a tapas bar on your way home for lunch or dinner and have a *vinito*, a little glass of wine, or *cañita*, a short beer, with just one small tapa taste. However, if you go out with some friends with the plan of stopping in several bars, then you're *de tapeo*, on a tapas crawl. Over the course of an evening, tapas and accompanying drinks add up to supper. In the Basque Country, the tapeo is *ir de pintxos*, to go for pintxos, which is the Basque word for small-bite foods.

Bar-hopping is *el copeo, chiquiteo, chateo* or *poteo*, terms derived from different words for a wine glass. In Galicia, it's *tomar una taza*, to have a "cuppa", because wine used to be served in small, white porcelain cups with no handles.

In Britain and America tapas are usually interpreted as small-plate dining, a series of dishes to be shared at the table. But, on home ground, in Spain, tapas are not really an alternative way of dining. For one thing, you might never sit at a table to have tapas. You stand at the bar or at little side tables, a window ledge, an upended barrel, any place to set a wine glass and small plate. And, you may or may not consume a quantity of tapas that adds up to a whole meal.

The tapeo is a movable feast—you stop at one bar to taste its specialty, then stroll up the street to another, around the corner for a third round. When you bump into another group of friends, you move on to a different locale. Part of the attraction of the tapeo is the *paseo*, stroll, and the *movida*, the action, the buzz. The movement is part of the entertainment. Spaniards will tell you that tapas will never really take off in other countries until you find two or more tapa bars within walking distance.

Part of the tapas protocol is that you eat them standing up. In many popular tapa bars, space is at a premium—there's no room for tables. So, you stand at the bar.

Where can you expect to sample tapas? Many tapa bars are like your local friendly neighbourhood pub, where you might stop off for a *copa* of wine, instead of a pint; enjoy a few bites of local sausage, listen to the evening news or stay on for the football game. *Bar* means a bar or pub, while a *barra* is the actual bar-top, of wood, zinc, stainless steel or tile, where the tapas are displayed.

In addition to bars, you can go for tapas to a *taberna* or *tasca* (both words for tavern), a *bodega* (barrel room or wine cellar), a *cervecería* (beer bar), a *sidrería* or *chigre* (cider house), a *champañería* (where cava or Champagne is served), a *marisquería* (where shellfish is served), a *freiduría* (fry shop), a

small-bites concept provides chefs a showcase for their latest culinary creations and allows diners to sample a wide range of dishes—a sort of tasting menu—without spending a lot of money.

Tapas are not necessarily finger-food, as some stews and sauced foods may require a spoon or fork plus bread for mopping up delicious sauces. But you should be able to eat them standing up, with just one hand.

The tapas experience is not just about the food and drink. It's about conviviality. Going out for tapas is a social event, so you need a little gang, a *cuadrilla*, of three, four or five people, for a proper tapas crawl. Each pays for a round of drinks and tapas. You may order a second round or move on to another bar. Animated chatter, gossip, shop talk, joke telling, cinema commentary, football league rehash, flirting—it's all part of the tapas scene. It's ok to exclaim over an especially good wine, but not to swirl and sniff and make a big deal of imbibing. Good wines, yes, but save the exquisite ones for occasions other than the tapeo.

When the weather is fine, the tapa scene spills outdoors and becomes part of street life. Some bars place high, stand-up tables on the pavement. You get your wine and plates of food at the bar, then regroup outside. What a good place to see and be seen, to keep an eye on who's coming and going!

Tapas have their pace, which is leisurely. Spaniards can put away quite a lot of food while just standing at the bar, sipping wine and having an animated conversation with friends. Enjoying the pure essence of Spanish life.

mesón or restaurant that also has a bar. A wine bar, *vinoteca*, probably serves tapas, usually paired with wine selections, but a *bar de copas*, cocktail bar, does not. Many *cafés* morph into tapa bars once the breakfast trade is finished.

So, what's for tapas? The variety is stunning. You can sample lots of flavours without eating large quantities of food, so they make a great introduction to Spanish food. You can choose foods in any order you like, eat meat and fish in any combination. Tapa bars serve from 10 to 50 different dishes, although some specialise in variations on a single theme. So, a particular bar may serve only ham and sausages; another, only bacalao (salt cod) dishes; others, exclusively shellfish, or snails.

Tapas range from very traditional home cooking to the innovative and trendy. The

A Tapas Tour of Spain

Though Andalusian in origin, tapas belong to every region of Spain. Their style and flavour change considerably from south to north and west to east. Here's a whirlwind tasting tour through all of Spain's provinces.

Andalusia. Made up of eight provinces, Sevilla, Córdoba, Jaén, Granada, Almería, Málaga, Cádiz and Huelva, this huge region extends across the southern quarter of the country.

The city of Sevilla is the capital of Andalusia and it may well be the tapas capital of the world. There is no more quintessential tapa experience than sipping a dry *fino manzanilla* (Sherry made in Sanlucar de Barrameda), peeling a tiger prawn and savouring a Sevilla olive in the cool interior of a Sevilla bar adorned with typical Sevilla tile work.

Sevilla, like every Spanish city or even village, is divided into barrios, districts, each known for its distinctive ambience and its tapa specialties. The Barrio Santa Cruz, with its narrow streets, is home to dozens of tapa bars with authentic flavours. Try *pavías de bacalao*, batter-fried strips of cod, and *espinacas con garbanzos*, spinach and chickpea stew. Avenida and Sierpes districts cover the city centre and extend as far as the Maestranza bullring. They include some of the old, polished tapas establishments, where local politicos might stop in for a Sherry and a small dish of home-style lentils and sausage. Triana, on the other side of the river, is full of local flamenco character and a good place to sample *caracoles*, snails in a piquant sauce.

Jerez is in Cádiz province, where seafood tapas are ideal with Sherry. (Although, if the truth be told, even in the hallowed land of Jerez, home of Sherry, not everyone sips the noble fino. Tapas go equally well with frosty draught beer.) Bars in Cádiz, Jerez, El Puerto de Santa María and Sanlucar serve seafood boiled, deep-fried, grilled, casseroled and baked.

Córdoba is another great tapas town. The province has its own wines, those of Montilla-Moriles, which are similar in style to Sherry. Try *salmorejo*, a thick gazpacho cream with a garnish of ham, and *flamenquines*, fried pork and cheese rolls. Málaga has bodegas in the town centre where Muscatel wines are dispensed from the barrel. They're so good with a platter of sliced sausage. Granada, perhaps because it is a university town, keeps up the tradition of serving free tapas with every drinks order. A good way to feed yourself for not much money!

Madrid. Life in Madrid would not be the same without the convivial rituals of the tapeo, the meeting and greeting, eating and imbibing. Besides being a sprawling city of many distinct neighbourhoods (Cava Baja and Plaza Santa Ana are two known for tapa bars), it is also the nation's capital and the centre of political, intellectual and artistic life. The

city's tascas reflect this diversity. Traditionally, they were gathering places where the intelligentsia met to talk—and drink and eat. Some establishments still display pronounced affiliations—political, *taurino* for bullfight aficionados, flamenco, literary, fans of Real Madrid football club and so on.

Because Madrid is the capital, it also has tapas outposts from every other region of Spain. You can find bars serving authentic Galician empanada, fried fish from Cádiz or paella from Valencia. La Mancha and its wines are deeply embedded in Madrid's tapa culture. Since the 19th century, they were the wines of choice for the taverns of Madrid, supplied by muleteers who hauled them to the capital in wineskins. With the coming of the railroad in 1861, a daily "wine train" delivered carloads of wine to the capital.

Madrid today is a sophisticated and cosmopolitan city where you will find everything from rustic taverns and traditional tapas (be sure to try *callos a la madrileña*, a lusty tripe stew) to franchise tapa bars that specialise in pintxo-style foods to stylish bars where chefs prepare cutting-edge gourmet tapas. The newest trend is towards wine bars featuring selections of interesting new wines (Spain has lots), poured by the glass and paired with exciting tapas.

Castilla y León and Castilla-La Mancha. These two enormous regions extend across all of central Spain, with Madrid at their centre. Both are big wine producing areas, so it follows that tapas are an important way of life

in these provinces—Burgos, Soria, Segovia, Ávila, Salamanca, Zamora, Valladolid, Palencia and León in Castilla y León and Toledo, Guadalajara, Cuenca, Albacete and Ciudad Real in Castilla-La Mancha.

You'll find some of the best tapas in old-fashioned, wood-panelled *mesones*, restaurants with adjoining bars, and *asadores*, grill houses that specialise in roast meats. Outstanding dishes are *la comida de cuchara*, "spoon food," slow-cooked stews and potages with legumes, vegetables and sausages. Both regions produce important cheeses, notably Manchego and Zamorano, and sausages too. Looking for something a little different on the tapas trail? Try *zarajos*, strips of lamb tripe wrapped around skewers of grape vine and grilled over a wood fire.

Extremadura. Spain's far west (Badajoz and Cáceres provinces) has a big claim to fame in the tapas round-up. Most of the famous ibérico ham and sausages that are served in the poshest bars all over Spain come from Extremadura. Stop off at a bar in any small town in the region and you'll enjoy this high-quality product at local prices. Worth a trip. The region also produces some distinctive cheeses.

La Rioja, Navarra and Aragón. These inland regions of northern Spain are connected by geography and wine. La Rioja (Logroño) and Navarra (Pamplona) are both small provinces, but huge on the wine scale. Aragón (Huesca, Zaragoza and Teruel provinces) ropes in

four different wine denominations. And, where there's wine, there's good food in local taverns.

Because of the proximity to the Basque Country, tapas tend toward the pintxo style—bites on cocktail sticks. But, not entirely. Logroño has its own tapas style. Here, local favourites acquire unusual names, so *alpargata de jamón*, is "rope-soled sandal," a toasted slab of bread topped with ham. Zaragoza also plays with nomenclature—a *guardia civil*, a "cop", is the name of a mini sandwich with spicy peppers. In La Rioja, tapa bars offer a great selection of different wines, so you don't have to go to a winery for tastings. You can conduct your own wine tasting in any bar, ordering wine by the glass, then selecting tapas to pair with the wines.

Basque Country. Basques are famous for their passion for food and the passion translates to incredibly good noshing. In the Basque Country, tapas are called pintxos (although tapas here also include *cazuelitas*, or little ramekins of sauced food).

Bilbao has several areas known for tapas, but the Siete Calles branching off of Plaza Nueva in the Casco Viejo, old town, have the greatest concentration of good places for eating and drinking. Pintxos make a really great way to eat lunch—choose two or three from the bar's display, and you've done lunch. All are freshly made daily and, if to be served hot, they are popped in a microwave for a quick reheating. Be sure to try *chipirones en su tinta*, baby squid cooked in their own ink.

The pintxos scene in San Sebastian also centres around the old part of town, Parte Vieja, where several long-established bars continue to attract a faithful clientele—as well as tourists. San Sebastian, an old and aristocratic resort city, also has a reputation for the most avant-garde cooking in Spain. So, you can move from the archetypal pintxo, the Gilda (pickled chilli, olive and anchovy on a cocktail stick) to a layered fantasy of smoked eel, duck pâté and caramelised apple.

In Bilbao and San Sebastian taverns, order the local white wine, *txacolí*, to go with your pintxos. Your first sip will taste almost mouth-puckeringly sharp. But, have a bite of a pintxo, such as rich, unctuous *bacalao al pil pil*, salt cod in pil pil garlic sauce, and then sip the txacolí again. Now the wine, with its acidity and slight fizz, is magically transformed. Light and crisp, it's a perfect match for the food.

Galicia. Galicia, in the northwest corner of Spain, produces a very different white wine made from Albariño grapes. Dry and citrusy, it seems created especially to accompany the region's fabulous seafood—scallops, mussels, oysters, lobster, turbot, sardines. Oh, yes, and *percebes*, those weird goose barnacles, incredibly expensive because they are hard come by. Wine bars in Galicia display gargantuan tapas—a huge wheel of *empanada*, savoury pie; a whole leg of roast pork to be carved and served on bread rolls; whole cooked octopus with sprawling tentacles to be chopped and served doused with a piquant sauce. The best tapa bars of

Santiago de Compostela, a university town, are in the old town not far from the grand cathedral. Galicia's provincial capitals— Orense, Pontevedra, La Coruña and Lugo— also are great tapa trolling grounds.

Asturias. Asturias, on the Bay of Biscay, produces no wine, but grows a hundred or more varieties of apples. Thus, cider is the regional drink. The cider houses of Asturias invoke a whole ritual for imbibing. Just stop in one of Oviedo's *sidrerías* on Calle Gascona (known as "cider boulevard") to join the rites. The waiter holds the bottle high above his head and pours a stream of cider into a glass held below waist level. This aerates the cider, adding to its slight natural fizz. You drink it down, discarding any dregs into a bucket, trough or, sometimes, onto a sawdust floor. In some taverns, you share the same glass with your pals. Cider oxidizes rapidly, so it's always consumed fresh, within a year of when it's produced. Cider goes great with the rustic foods of Asturias, such as *fabada*, a bean and sausage stew, and with the local seafood. It's also used as a cooking ingredient—chorizo sausage simmered in cider or hake in a cider sauce are two great dishes.

Cantabria. In Santander taverns, order a cheese board with a selection of the regional cheeses. Also noteworthy is the *tortilla de setas*, tortilla of eggs and wild mushrooms. Choose wine from any region of Spain, as Cantabria produces hardly any.

Catalonia, Valencia and Murcia. These three regions stretch along the entire eastern Mediterranean coast of Spain. Catalonia includes the provinces of Barcelona, Girona, Lérida and Tarragona. The Valencia region includes the provinces of Valencia, Castellón de la Plana and Alicante, while Murcia is a single province.

These regions were latecomers to the tapa scene—but have quickly made up for lost time. Andalusians, who emigrated to Catalonia, are sometimes credited with establishing the first tapa bars in Barcelona. But, once the idea caught on, the Catalans made it their own, creating stylish bars and designer tapas for what is, arguably, Spain's most trend-setting city. Here "tradition" could mean last year's favourite dish and fusion is not a dirty word, so you might find tapas with an Asian influence—sushi paella or soy-roasted tuna. A delightful take on tapas when accompanied by Catalonia-made bubbly cava.

This is not to say that Barcelona doesn't have a down-to-earth side as well. Any neighbourhood bar will serve a fine *pa amb tomaquet*, Catalan lingo for toast rubbed with tomato, drizzled with (Catalan) olive oil and topped with serrano ham. And, should you fancy tapas for breakfast, head for Barcelona's fabulous Boquería market and grab a stool at one of several market bars, where you might rub shoulders with a famous chef. Order cava by the glass and sample real market cuisine— fish, meat and vegetables from the market stalls. Try the tapas of baby squid with broad beans, a salt cod salad called *esqueixada* or chickpeas stewed with Catalan black sausage.

Valencia is not so much of a tapas-on-the-hoof type city, as are Madrid and Sevilla. Here you might snag a table at a favourite bar and stay there through various rounds of drinks and tapas. While you might find paella served in small dishes as a tapa in other regions of Spain, in Valencia, home of paella, it's too sacrosanct for casual snacking. Nevertheless, Valencia bars offer a huge spectrum of tastes. Fresh anchovies are one of the best. Sample baby cuttlefish cooked on a griddle or *titaina*, a salad with dried tuna.

Murcia is famous for its vegetables and seafood. Try egg tortilla made with aubergines, peppers and tomatoes and *queso de Murcia al Vino*, a goat´s milk cheese cured in red wine.

Balearic Islands and Canary Islands. These archipelagos are Spain's off-shore assets. The Balearic Islands of Mallorca, Menorca and Ibiza are totally Mediterranean, while the Canaries are in the Atlantic off the coast of Morocco. All offer tapas "out of the mainstream," so to speak. The Canary Islands have the more exotic cuisine—look for wrinkly potatoes with *mojo*, a chilli-inflected sauce with coriander. The Balearic Islands, not too distant from Catalonia, have a special sausage, *sobreasada*, that's great spread on toast.

PLANNING A TAPAS PARTY

PLANNING A TAPAS PARTY

Loving those tapas in Spanish bars is one thing. But, how do you get the tapas from tasca to your table? That's what this cookbook is all about—showing you how to make delicious tapa dishes for parties in your own home.

Tapas, almost by definition, are bar food. Nevertheless, many of them translate very nicely to home entertaining. A spread of salads and cold dishes is very nice for a buffet dinner. Trays of finger foods—bites on bread or cocktail sticks, fritters and croquettes—can be passed as hors d'ouevres at a drinks party. Tortilla is great for brunch or picnic. Griddled foods are right at home at a barbecue. Many tapas can become starters, side dishes or main dishes, so you can adapt them to a dinner party. Often all you need to add is pudding or pastry to the tapas dishes to complete the menu plan.

Your personal style of entertaining should guide you in planning a tapas menu. Are you having a great big party, where everyone mills around on foot, or just a few friends over for drinks? A buffet meal? Dinner for six to eight or a gang around the barbecue on the terrace? There are tapa recipes to suit any occasion.

Here's a really simple party plan: just choose one tapa from each of the recipe chapters—Sausage, Ham and Cheese; Bites on Bread; Small Bites; Salads and Cold Dishes; Potato Tortilla and More Egg Dishes; Foods on the Griddle; Saucy Dishes; Out of the Frying Pan; Sauces, Dressings, Dips and Spreads, and What to Drink with Tapas. Some more detailed party menus appear at the end of this chapter.

Most tapas can be prepared before guests arrive, either to be served cold or quickly reheated. Recipes indicate make-ahead suggestions, where dishes can be cooked in advance, reheated or even frozen.

Here are a few considerations in planning your tapas party.

How to calculate quantities? For a drinks party (not dinner), figure on at least four different tapas to serve six to eight people. Each person will eat three or four of each one. Plan six to eight tapas for eight to 12 people. A guest will eat two or three of each. For big parties, more than 12 people, serve as many as 12 different tapas and expect each person to eat two or three.

Will your guests be seated or circulating on foot? If they're seated, you can present some tapas in individual small dishes with spoons or forks, so saucy foods work fine. But, guests on foot, with a wine glass in one hand, can only pick up tapas easily handled with one hand. Tapas on cocktail sticks or on bread are the best choices.

Consider your serving capacity. Do you have enough individual small dishes to go around? If not, plan tapas that can be picked up from a tray and don't require dishes. Do provide napkins, as even finger foods and pintxos can be a little messy. In Spain, you can buy inexpensive little *cazuelitas*, pottery dishes, for individual tapas, or use any

ramekins, small bowls or, now that no one smokes anymore, recycle ceramic ashtrays for tapa dishes.

Are tapas going to be the whole meal? This is tricky. A few friends sitting around, sipping wine, may arrive early and stay late. Even though the evening was never intended to include dinner, make the tapas substantial enough. If they want to go home and have an omelette later, that's fine. But, if it's a multitudinous drinks party, don't expect to feed guests a meal. Titillate their taste buds.

A tip: don´t put out all the tapas at once. Serve them two-by-two. If possible, provide a clean ramekin (or paper plate) for each tapa so that your guests don't have to pile them on a plate together.

Check out What to Drink with Tapas for lots of information about Spanish wines as well as some recipes for cocktails and wine coolers that might accompany tapas.

Following are tapa plans for various kinds of parties. Please see the Index to find the recipes.

A few friends for drinks.

These are tapas for a very small group (four to eight), where you're all sitting around, cosy by the fire in the winter or al fresco on the terrace in the summer. You can prepare most of the tapas in advance. Do the last-minute ones while your partner is opening the wines.

1. Beetroot, Cheese and Sausage Bites

    Olive Pâté on Toast, with Quail Eggs

    Cheese Puffs with Piquillo Red Pepper Sauce

    Meatballs in Almond Sauce

    The cheese puffs can be fried in advance and reheated in the oven. Serve the piquillo red pepper dipping sauce at room temperature. The meatballs can be prepared in advance and reheated in the microwave. Serve them in individual ramekins with cocktail sticks or forks and chunks of bread. This tapa selection goes well with red and white wines.

2. Fried Almonds

    Cheese in Olive Oil

    Ham Croquettes

    Shellfish Balls in Green Sauce

    Beef Fillet Tips with Sherry

    The croquettes can be prepared in advance, frozen, then fried before serving. Reheat them in a hot oven, if you like. The shellfish balls need dishes, but can be eaten with a cocktail stick. The beef fillet is cut in small chunks, speared on cocktail sticks. Serve this tapas selection with fino and amontillado Sherry or Montilla-Moriles wine.

Drinks party for 10 to 20.

Spanish tapas are perfect for parties like this. Serve the tapas two-by-two, not all at once. Most of them can be passed or picked up from a tray.

White Gazpacho Shooters with Grapes

Chickpea Salad with Sausage

Mussels Vinaigrette

Stuffed Mushrooms

Garlicky Salt Cod Spread on Toast

Aubergine Tortilla

Vegetable Medley on Toast

Seared Quail Breasts with Dates

Fried Chicken Wings with Cabrales Blue Cheese Sauce

Serve the white gazpacho in shot glasses. The chickpea salad requires a dish and fork or spoon. Both the seared quail breasts and the fried chicken wings can be prepared before party time and served at room temperature. Chicken wings are a bit messy, so provide paper napkins plus a bin for tossing the bones. Accompany the tapas with red and white wines, beer and soft drinks.

Buffet dinner for a celebration.

This is perfect for a New Year's Day open house or a grand birthday celebration. You can adapt the menu to serve from 15 to 40. Choose a main dish to centre the buffet, such as pre-cooked ham, turkey, roast pork or whole salmon, and add tapas to accompany it. Some can be passed as hors d'oeuvres. Most will be served as side dishes on the buffet table. Provide dinner plates, with knives and forks, as needed.

Cava Cocktail

Sliced Serrano or Ibérico Ham

Quince Paste with Cheese

Partridge Pâté

Fried Pasties with Tuna Filling

Lollipops of Quail in Escabeche Marinade

Shellfish Cocktail

Málaga Salad with Oranges and Olives

Cauliflower Salad with Olives

Potato Casserole

Fry the tuna pasties before party time. Reheat them in the oven shortly before serving. The potato casserole, a wonderful side dish, can be prepared in advance and reheated in the oven before serving.

PLANNING A TAPAS PARTY

Sunday brunch.

Here's an easygoing menu for six to eight persons.

"Valencia Water" (Orange Juice and Cava)

Blood Sausage with Apple

Smoked Mackerel on Toast

Spinach Fritters

Sausage Bites in Sherry

Kidneys in Sherry Sauce

"Dismantled" Eggs with Baby Broad Beans and Ham

Mini Rolls

Summer barbecue.

Fire up the charcoal and get grilling. Most of the recipes in Foods on the Griddle can be adapted for the barbecue. And, many in Salads and Cold Dishes make great side dishes with barbecue foods.

White Wine Coolers

Figs with Ham

Gazpacho in a Glass

Swordfish Kebabs

Mini Kebabs with Moorish Spices

Roasted Aubergines and Peppers

Potato Salad with Lemon Dressing

Instead of cutting the swordfish into appetiser-sized kebabs, cook whole steaks. The pork mini-kebabs, though, are best skewered. Use fresh, not dried, figs with the ham.

Dinner party.

Here are two dinner party menus. Look under Main Dishes in the Index for more tapas that can be adapted to a dinner menu. Add cake, pudding, fruit or ice cream for dessert.

1. Aubergine (Eggplant) and Prawn Rollups

    Scallop Gratin

    Seared Duck Breast with Two Sauces

    Mushroom and Artichoke Mélange

    Potatoes with Importance

    An Albariño wine from Rías Baixas would complement both the fried aubergine-prawn rolls and the scallop gratin. Choose a red reserva wine to go with the duck.

2. Wheat Crisps with Green Chilli Sauce with Coriander

    Griddled Vegetables

    Rice and Seafood, Seville Style

    The wheat crisps and green chilli dip can be made days in advance. The griddled vegetables can be prepared before dinner and served room temperature, or cooked immediately before serving.This rice dish is similar to paella, but it cooks in a cazuela, an earthenware casserole. Pour a fresh rosé wine and invite your dinner guests into the kitchen to keep you company while it cooks.

La Tabla

SAUSAGE, HAM & CHEESE

La Tabla
SAUSAGE, HAM & CHEESE

Partridge Pâté (*Paté de Perdiz*)

Pickled Aubergine (*Berenjenas en Escabeche*)

A Tasting Guide to Spanish Sausages

The Whole Ham Story

The Cheese Board

Cheese in Olive Oil (*Queso al Aceite de Oliva*)

Duck into a tasca on the plaza and belly-up to the bar. Order a *cañita*, a short draught beer. And, for a tapa? Right in front of you is a line-up of sausages—six or more fat rolls, with colours from pink to red to orange to black, ready to be sliced to order and served on a *tabla*, a board or platter. Order a *surtido* and you get a mixed selection of sausages to sample.

You can order a selection of ordinary sausages or sausages made from the highly esteemed ibérico breed of pig (see The Whole Ham Story, page 42). Expect anything ibérico to cost a lot more than ordinary sausages.

Behind the bar hang whole hams, dangling from their trim black hooves, pedigrees attached. One ham is clamped on a special rack. A bartender wielding a long, thin knife cuts paper-thin slices of the ham when you place your order. He carefully arranges them on a plate or board and serves the ham accompanied by bread.

At the other end of the bar, whole rounds of cheese are lined up beneath a glass case. Bookending the cheese display is an oversized jar filled with sliced cheese immersed in extra virgin olive oil. Fished out and placed on sliced bread, the cheese in oil is a ready-made tapa.

Sausages, ham and cheese are the principal choices for a tabla, or board. Some tapa bars might also offer a selection of pâtés, such as partridge, boar and goose liver (buy these in tins or at the deli counter of your supermarket), or of *ahumados*, smoked fish, including salmon, cod and trout. Some other interesting "cold cuts" are *cecina*, raw, salt-cured beef or venison, served, like ham, in thin slices; and *mojama*, "ham of the sea," salt-cured tuna and tuna roe, thinly sliced and drizzled with a little extra virgin olive oil and freshly ground black pepper.

A tabla always comes with bread. Additionally, pickled foods such as olives, capers, caper berries, gherkins, chillies and pickled aubergine (eggplant) make great accompaniments. You can complement a cheese board with contrasting sweet flavours, such as *dulce de membrillo*, quince paste; *cabello de angel*, candied "angel's hair" squash; and *pan de higos*, fig roll; as well as fresh fruit and nuts.

After that introductory beer, you may want to switch to dry Sherry or robust red wine to accompany the tabla of your choice. While it may seem counter-intuitive, medium-sweet Málaga Muscatel goes extremely well with sausages and pâté, while dry, white wine pairs with many Spanish cheeses.

Paté de Perdiz
PARTRIDGE PÂTÉ

You might sample this delectable pâté in a Toledo tasca, because Toledo is famous for its partridge. You can substitute pork, veal or more chicken for the partridge.

Serves 16 to 20.

450 g / 1 lb boned partridge (or pork, veal or chicken)
450 g / 1 lb boned chicken
225 g / 8 oz fresh pork belly *(panceta fresca)*
2 eggs, separated
120 ml / 4 fl oz / ½ cup milk
4 tablespoons brandy
4 tablespoons dry or medium Sherry

1 tablespoon salt
225 g / 8 oz chicken livers
1 teaspoon freshly ground black pepper
½ teaspoon dried thyme
4 tablespoons finely chopped flat-leaf parsley
½ onion, grated
15 g / ½ ounce black truffles, chopped (optional)

Cut the partridge, chicken, and pork belly into cubes. Mince the meat in two batches in a processor or blender, adding 1 egg yolk and 4 tablespoons milk to each batch.

Combine the paste in a bowl with the brandy, Sherry, and salt. Chop the chicken livers in the processor or blender and mix thoroughly into the paste. Season with pepper, thyme, parsley, and onion. Allow the mixture to stand, covered and refrigerated, for at least 1 hour or up to 8 hours.

Preheat oven to 180ºC / 350ºF.

Beat the egg whites until stiff. Stir a third of the whites into the partridge paste. Fold remaining whites into the paste.

Place half the mixture in a loaf pan (or in two smaller terrine moulds). Scatter the chopped truffle on top, if using. Spread the remaining pâté mixture over. Place the mould in a pan and fill to half the depth with boiling water. Cover the top with foil. Bake until pâté is set, internal temperature of 85ºC / 180ºF, about 1 hour (50 minutes for the smaller terrines).

Allow the pâté to cool, then refrigerate. Unmould the pâté, draining off excess liquid, and slice to serve.

Berenjenas en Escabeche
PICKLED AUBERGINE

This is an unusual pickle, good served with cold cuts. In Spain, buy it in tins. The pickled aubergines (eggplant) are made with tiny, round, green aubergines. Speared on short lengths of wild fennel, they are pickled whole, with stems attached. The aubergines are served, like olives, as a tapa. You pick them up by the stem and eat the nubbin of aubergine.

This recipe is an adaptation and is not meant to be a conserve. Keep it, refrigerated, up to 3 weeks. If you serve the aubergine as an aperitif, spear the pieces with cocktail sticks.

Makes about 950 ml / 1 ½ pints / 4 cups pickles.

2 medium aubergines (eggplant)
(680 g / 1 ½ lbs)
Salt
2 tablespoons sweet pimentón (paprika)
½ teaspoon cayenne
1 tablespoon ground cumin

½ teaspoon fennel seed
¼ teaspoon cinnamon
6 tablespoons white wine vinegar
½ lemon, sliced, to serve
2 tablespoons olive oil, to serve

Peel the aubergines. Cut them lengthwise into quarters, then slice crosswise into 35-mm / 1 ½-in wedges.

Bring a large pan of water to the boil with 3 tablespoons salt. Have ready a pan of ice water. Add the aubergine pieces to the boiling water. When water returns to the boil, cook the aubergine 2 minutes. Drain and plunge into ice water. When cooled, drain well.

In a bowl combine the pimentón, cayenne, cumin, fennel, cinnamon, and ½ teaspoon salt. Stir the vinegar into the spices until smooth. Add this mixture to 350 ml / 12 fl oz /1 ½ cups water in a saucepan. Bring to the boil and cook 1 minute. Add the aubergine and bring again to the boil. Remove the pan from the heat.

Place the aubergine and liquid in a heatproof bowl or jar. Cover tightly. When cool, refrigerate. Aubergine is ready to eat in 24 hours. It keeps, refrigerated, up to 3 weeks. Serve the aubergine pieces garnished with lemon slices and drizzled with olive oil.

■ A TASTING GUIDE TO SPANISH SAUSAGES

***Chacina* is pork butchery and sausages, the same as French *charcuterie*. *Embutidos* means sausages. Most Spanish sausages are known by their proper names.**

Butifarra blanca. A Catalan smooth-textured white sausage made of minced pork and spices, which is cooked before curing. Good for barbecuing, it can also be sliced and fried or simmered in soups.

Chorizo. This is Spain's most emblematic sausage. It's made from chopped or minced pork meat and fat, sometimes with beef as well, macerated with sweet and hot pimentón (paprika) or the pulp from *choricero* peppers, plus pepper, garlic and oregano. After stuffing in casings, the sausages are air-dried. Lactic fermentation gives the sausage a distinctive tangy flavour.

There are actually two types of chorizo, although, if you are shopping for ingredients outside of Spain, you may find only the dry-cured variety. "Soft" chorizo is tied off into short links, *en ristra*. It has more fat content than hard chorizo and is semi-cured. Soft chorizo is for stewing, grilling or frying. Dry-cured chorizo, while it can be used in cooking too, is meant to be served sliced as a cold cut. It comes in several shapes, such as thick rolls, *cular*, or thinner "candle" ones, *vela*.

Pamplona chorizo is a version that is more finely chopped. *Chistorra* is a skinny loop of Pamplona-type chorizo. Chorizo from Asturias, in northern Spain, is smoke-dried. There is also chorizo made from *jabalí*, wild boar.

Lomo embuchado. Whole pork loin, seasoned with spices, is stuffed in wide casings and cured. Also known as *caña de lomo*, this is the aristocrat of sausages.

Longaniza. This refers to any long, skinny sausage served as a cold cut.

Morcilla. Blood sausage, black pudding. Made with pig's blood, minced pork fat and meat and spices, the sausage is boiled, then air-dried. Each region has a different version, spiced with cinnamon, cloves, nutmeg, anise and containing onion, rice, pine nuts. Especially well-known types of morcilla come from Burgos, where it is made with rice; from Ronda, with onions; and from Asturias, smoked.

Morcilla is usually stewed, but it can be barbecued or eaten cold.

Morcón. A thick sausage made of diced pieces of meat and fat packed into wide casings.

Chorizo. **This is Spain's most emblematic sausage**

Morcilla. **Blood sausage, black pudding.**

Salchichón. A hard-cured sausage, somewhat like salami. Thin ones may be called *fuet* or *longaniza*. Longaniza de Vic is a variety in which the meat and fat are a homogenous grind.

Sobreasada. A soft, fatty, spreadable sausage from Mallorca, flavoured similarly to chorizo. Spread it, like butter, on slabs of hot, toasted bread.

■ THE WHOLE HAM STORY

You order a *copita* of fino Sherry and a small plate of ham to accompany it. "Which ham do you want?" asks the barman. "What's the difference?" you ask.

The most obvious difference is in price. A plate of ibérico ham will cost you about ten times more than a plate of serrano ham. The reason for this is that ibérico ham derives from the ibérico breed of pig, raised in limited quantities, fed on natural forage and artisanally cured. Serrano ham comes from regular pigs, raised on an industrial scale and cured in big meat-processing plants.

Spain produces the most cured hams in the world—some 33.5 million pieces annually, including both cured hams and shoulders. Serrano represents about 90 percent of Spanish ham production.

Ibérico Ham

Ibérico pigs, descended from the wild boar that once roamed Mediterranean lands, are built like little barrels on slim legs. They have big ears to shade their eyes from fierce sun and long snouts, the better for rooting. Ibérico pigs are the colour of earth. Many—but not all—have black hooves, thus the popular name, *pata negra*.

The breed plus its natural habitat, the *dehesa*, account for the extraordinary quality of the cured ham. The dehesa is a unique ecosystem of rolling meadowland, interspersed with stands of wild holm and cork oaks, that exists only in western Spain. The ibérico breed developed in this habitat, adapting to dry summers of little forage by storing fat infiltrated in the flesh during the *montanera*, the season of foraging for *bellotas*, wild acorns.

During the montanera fattening period, the pigs range freely through the dehesa, feeding on fallen acorns, grass, roots, bulbs, herbs. One hog eats about 8 kg / 18 pounds of acorns per day, increasing its weight by almost 50 percent in the months before slaughter. The number of pigs raised is limited by the available acorns. In a year of poor supply, some stock is separated to be finished on *recebo*, pig feed and grain. (Ham labels indicate whether the hog was finished on bellota, acorn, or recebo. Bellota hams are the most expensive of all.)

After butchering, the hams are packed in salt and stacked for 10 to 12 days, depending on their weight.

The hams are brushed free of salt and washed in clear water. They are sent next to a cold locker, where temperature and humidity are stabilized. Then the hams are hung, one by one, in a drying hall situated in the attic. Shutters keep out the sun and

let in the air. Hams hang here throughout the summer. During hot weather, the fat liquefies slightly, bathing the meat in flavour.

At the end of the summer the hams are transferred to the *bodega*, a dim cellar with thick walls where humidity encourages the growth of *flor*, a mould that contributes to the curing process. Like fine wine and cheese, hams mature and develop flavour and complex bouquet during this ageing process, which lasts 12 months or more.

The hams are ready to eat at this point (although some are aged even longer). They are not smoked, soaked, nor cooked. Ibérico ham, because it is produced in limited quantity, remains one of those gourmet products, like caviar, truffles and foie gras, that commands very high prices. It's meant to be enjoyed on special occasions, not simply slapped on a ham sandwich.

Allow the ham to warm on your tongue, releasing its unique aroma and flavour, sweet and subtly nutty, succulent and not in the least salty. Have a sip of Sherry.

Serrano Ham

Serrano means "mountain," so-called because these hams traditionally were produced in upland regions of the country where dry summers and cold winters enhanced the curing process. Climate once controlled the process, but now computer-controlled refrigeration and drying chambers mimic the conditions of four seasons.

Serrano hams come from white pigs such as Duroc, Landrace and Large White that are fed on cereal-based pig feed and slaughtered at seven to eight months, weighing about 135 kg / 300 pounds. These hams are heavier and broader than ibérico hams.

The hams are packed in salt for approximately one day per kilo (2.2 pounds) of weight. The hams are next washed free of salt, tied by the hocks and hung on racks. Temperature is gradually raised, through "springtime" temperatures to warmer "summer" ones. As humidity is gradually lowered, air circulation aids in the slow dehydration process. Moulds begin to form on the surface of the hams, indicating the transformation to cured meat.

Serving Spanish Ham

Properly slicing serrano or ibérico ham from the bone requires expertise. To best release its flavour and aroma, the ham should be sliced almost paper-thin. However, boned, sliced and vacuum-packed products simplify serving.

Remove packaged ham from the refrigerator 20 minutes before serving, allowing it to come to room temperature.

Spread the slices on a plate in a single layer. If purchasing ham at a deli counter where it is sliced from a whole ham, keep it tightly wrapped and use as soon as possible. Ham exposed to air begins to dry and lose its aromatic qualities.

Serve Spanish ham as an aperitif with bread to accompany it. Try it with *pan catalán* (page 56), thick slabs of country bread, toasted, rubbed with garlic and fresh tomato pulp, drizzled with extra virgin olive oil and topped with sliced ham. It makes a good breakfast or tapa.

Ham pairs beautifully with sweet melon; wraps spears of asparagus, or, cut in strips, tops a thick "gazpacho cream," called *salmorejo* (page 252). Scatter strips of ham over a salad of sliced oranges, onions and olives and drizzle with extra virgin olive oil.

Ham loses its delicacy of flavour and texture with cooking. However, used as "seasoning," it lends character to sautéed vegetables (sensational with mushrooms), omelettes, lentil and bean dishes, prawns. Just sauté the chopped ham very briefly in a little olive oil and combine with the other ingredients at the end of cooking. Add chopped ham to hot consommé with a dash of Sherry and garnish the soup with fresh mint.

■ THE CHEESE BOARD

With more than 100 different regional cheeses, Spain is second only to France in diversity of cheeses. Some are so distinctive that they have *denominación de origen* (DO) labels. Some are hardly marketed outside their region of production, while others are produced on an industrial scale and are widely available in Spain and abroad. Manchego, for example, seems to be the next Gruyère in world popularity.

Spain's cheeses may be made from the milk of cows, sheep or goats or a mixture of all three. In general, cows' milk cheeses come from the northern third of the country, where green pastures allow dairy cattle to thrive; sheep's milk cheeses from the middle of the country, through the sheep-rearing regions of Castilla-La Mancha and Castilla y León, and goats' milk cheeses from Andalusia, Extremadura and Murcia.

Serve cheese with wine or Sherry and a selection of bread or crackers. Good accompaniments are fruit, walnuts, quince paste.

Here's a sampling.

SHEEP'S MILK CHEESES

Manchego. Produced in the central Castilla-La Mancha region, Manchego is Spain's best-known cheese. True Manchego, with DO, is made only in the designated geographical region and from the milk of Manchega-breed ewes. It must be aged a minimum of 60 days for semi-cured, producing a mild, smooth cheese with a subtle nutty aroma, delicious served on its own or used in cooking. Aged Manchego can be fairly piquant and the well-aged is splintery, strong, but mellow. Artisanal cheese is made from raw milk; industrial cheese is made from pasteurised milk. DO.

Idiazábal. Made from the milk of the long-haired *latxa* sheep in the Basque Country. It is a robust, slightly acidic cheese that is often smoked over beechwood. DO.

Roncal. From Navarrese valleys in the Pyrenees. Aged a minimum of four months, it is buttery, earthy. DO.

La Serena and *Torta de Casar.* Both from Extremadura and both unusual in that they are made with a vegetable coagulant, a kind of thistle. La Serena is a creamy cheese, expensive because it is made in very small quantities. Torta de Casar is a soft, runny cheese with a slight bitter taste. To serve, the top rind is opened and the cheese scooped out with a spoon. DO.

Zamorano. Made in Zamora province in Castilla y León region from the milk of *churra* and *castellana* sheep. Long-aged in cellars and rubbed with oil, it is intense, nutty, slightly piquant. DO.

■ GOATS' MILK CHEESES

Garrotxa. Semi-soft Catalan cheese.

Ibores. Made from raw goats' milk in Cáceres (Extremadura). It has a dark rind, buttery texture, wild herb flavour. DO.

Majorero. From Fuerteventura in the Canary Islands. Usually rubbed with oil and pimentón (paprika). Acidic, a little piquant, buttery. DO.

Málaga and ***Ronda.*** Fresh white goats' cheese from the mountains near Ronda (Málaga). It is mild, slightly salty and is also semi-cured.

Murcia al vino. From Murcia in eastern Spain, a soft, white goat cheese bathed in red wine, giving it a purple rind and a tangy flavour. DO.

COWS' MILK AND MIXED MILK CHEESES

Afuega'l pitu. Asturias. A crumbly cheese, slightly acidic, sometimes with pimentón (paprika) added. DO.

Arzúa-Ulloa. Galicia. Yellowish cheese, smooth, slightly elastic curd. The cured cheese is slightly acidic with a bitter butter aroma. DO.

Burgos. Fresh, mild, moist white cheese from Burgos. It is good with honey and walnuts.

Cabrales. A blue cheese from Asturias in northern Spain. Aged in caves, it is off-white, veined with blue-green. It has a lovely creamy consistency with a bit of a "bite" to it. DO.

Cantabria. Melt-in-the-mouth creamy cheese with a bittersweet flavour. DO.

Cebreiro. Galicia. Firm, yellow cheese, slightly piquant.

Alt Urgell and ***Cerdanya***. Made from pasteurised cows' milk in the Catalan Pyrenees. These cheeses have an amber-coloured rind and soft, creamy flesh. DO.

Gamonedo. Mixed-milk cheese from Asturias. It is a blue cheese, lightly smoked with a buttery texture and hazelnut flavour. DO.

Mahón. Made on the island of Menorca. Can be fresh, semi-cured or well aged, in which case it is quite piquant. The rind may be rubbed with oil and pimentón (paprika). DO.

Picón. Cantabria. Often made with a mixture of cows', sheep's and goat's milk. Aged in caves, a blue-veined cheese. DO.

Quesucos de Liébana. Cantabria, three-milk cheese; sometimes smoked. DO.

Tetilla. From Galicia in northwest Spain, the cheese is named for its shape, a lovely rounded breast. Yellow on the outside, paler on the inside, with a smooth, buttery texture. Very mild. DO. ***San Simón*** is a similar cheese that is smoked, giving it a darker, oiler rind and smoky flavour.

Valdeón. A smooth and mild blue cheese from the Picos de Europa area of León. It is a cows' milk cheese that sometimes has goats' milk added. DO.

Villalón. A soft, fresh mild cheese from Castilla y León.

Queso al Aceite de Oliva
CHEESE IN OLIVE OIL

Submerging cheese in olive oil is a way to preserve cut cheese and prevent its drying out. It also adds flavour. Use a semi-cured cheese, such as Manchego or Roncal. Rosemary is a strongly-flavoured herb. Use it only if you really like it. Use the cheese in salads or served with bread or on toast. Dribble some of the oil over the salad or bread.

225 g / 8 oz cheese, sliced in triangles 15 mm / ⅜ in thick
Extra virgin olive oil to cover, about 300 ml / ½ pint / 1 ¼ cups
⅛ teaspoon dried thyme
4 peppercorns
1 bay leaf
2 sprigs fresh rosemary (optional)

Pack the sliced cheese into a wide-mouthed glass or ceramic jar. Pour over enough oil to completely cover the cheese. Add thyme, peppercorns, bay and rosemary, if using. Cover tightly.

Refrigerate at least 5 days. Cheese keeps up to 2 months.

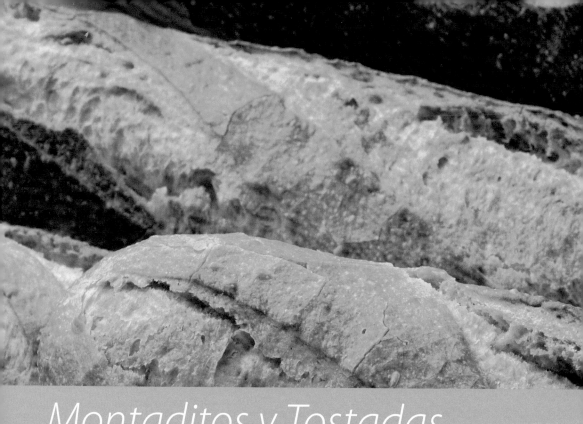

Montaditos y Tostadas

BITES ON BREAD

Montaditos y Tostadas
BITES ON BREAD

Catalan Toasts (*Pan Catalán*)

Marinated Pork Loin on Toast (*Montaditos de Lomo en Adobo*)

Blood Sausage with Raisins and Pine Nuts on Toast (*Montadito de Morcilla*)

Ham and Eggs on Toast (*Cojonudo*)

Sardine Pâté on Toast (*Paté de Sardinas*)

Smoked Mackerel on Toast (*Caballa Ahumada con Tostas*)

Salt Cod and Roasted Pepper on Toast (*Tiznao*)

Garlicky Salt Cod Spread on Toast (*Brandada de Bacalao*)

Mini Roll with Spicy Sardines (*Mini de Sardinas Picantes*)

Mini Roll with Tuna (*Capote con Atún*)

Roasted Aubergines and Peppers (*Escalivada*)

Mushroom and Artichoke Mélange (*Menestra con Setas y Alcachofas*)

Mini Pizzas with Two Toppings (*Coques*)

Empanada with Tuna Filling (*Empanada de Bonito*)

Basic Bread Dough

Mini Rolls and Maxi Rolls (*Bollitos y Molletes*)

Toasts (*Tostas y Tostadas*)

Wheat Crisps (*Regañás*)

montaditos y tostadas
BITES ON BREAD

All tapas are served with bread. But a tapa that's served atop a slice of bread or toast becomes a category of its own. This includes open-faced sandwiches, toast with toppings, canapés, sandwiches on bread rolls and fillings baked with the bread. They range from titbits to substantial lunch entrées. Here's the line-up.

Montaditos. Means "mounted," or "up in the saddle." A slice of juicy, fried pork loin on top of a slice of bread or toast is a classic montadito. Top with a strip of red piquillo pepper, for colour and flavour. You can heap just about anything on bread and call it a montadito—for example, Russian salad (page 105), fried fish (page 213), sautéed mushrooms (page 162). So, go ahead, invent some montadito combos for yourself.

Tostadas y tostas. Toasts and toasts—these are, basically, the same thing, although the size can vary from generous to teensy. Spread the toast with a savoury topping—such as olive oil, tomato and ham or a smooth pâté—to make a variety of tapas. Some of these might look a lot like what you used to call canapés. They're easy, do-ahead appetisers for a drinks party. Others, such as Catalan toasts, made with thick slabs of country bread, you'll see being consumed for breakfast in all the classy cafés.

Bocaditos, bocadillos, minis, ligeritos, pitufos, molletes. These are variations on the sandwich theme. They may be mini rolls or crusty buns with various fillings. These are great for lunch or packed on picnics. A *bollo* is a crusty roll, split for a sandwich, which is called *bocadito* or *bocadillo*. A *bollito* is a smaller roll, used for a *pitufo* sandwich. Mini and *ligerito* are tiny buns, usually with soft crusts, while *mollete* is a soft, flat bap of a bun, somewhere between a pita and hamburger bun.

Empanadas, empanadillas. These are pastries with savoury fillings. Big *empanadas*, served by the slice, are usually made with bread dough. They make great picnic food. *Empanadillas* are small, filled pastries or pasties, made with a short crust instead of bread dough (recipe page 74).

Coques. Catalan pizzas—slabs of bread dough with savoury toppings, baked until crust is browned.

While most fillings and toppings for bites on bread are dead-easy to prepare—how hard is it to open a tin?—a few classics require a host of ingredients and long, slow cooking. One such is *pringá*, an Andalusian specialty. To make this tapa, first you have to prepare a slow-cooked *cocido* or *puchero*, with fatty pork, ham, sausages, beef shin, chicken and vegetables. The leftover bits of fat pork and sausages are chopped up together and spread in a toasted mini roll. Look for this tapa in Sevilla and Cádiz.

Pan Catalán
CATALAN TOASTS

The Catalans call this *pa amb tomaquet*, bread with tomato, but elsewhere in Spain it's known as "Catalan toasts." Serve it for breakfast with *café con leche* or as a tapa with wine. At its best, the toasts are prepared individually—the bread toasted over a wood fire, then scrubbed with a cut tomato to impregnate it with the juices. But if you're serving a party, toast the bread under a grill and prepare the tomato pulp in advance.

Serves 8.

8 thick slices country bread
1 or 2 ripe tomatoes
1 clove garlic, cut in half
3 tablespoons extra virgin olive oil
Thinly sliced serrano or ibérico ham

Toast the bread under a grill, over a wood fire or in the toaster. Cut the tomato in half crosswise and grate it coarsely, discarding the skin. Rub each toast with a cut clove of garlic and spread the tomato pulp on top. Drizzle each with a teaspoon of oil. Arrange the sliced ham on top. Serve immediately.

Montaditos de Lomo en Adobo
MARINATED PORK LOIN ON TOAST

A tapa or a lunch – juicy pork loin mounted on bread is the perfect snack with a cold draught beer.

Makes 12 tapas or 6 lunch servings.

12 slices pork loin, 12 mm / ½ in thick (about 900 g / 2 lb)
½ teaspoon salt
Coarsely ground black pepper
1 teaspoon oregano
½ teaspoon pimentón (paprika)
4 cloves coarsely chopped garlic
2 bay leaves, broken into pieces
4 cloves
1 tablespoon vinegar
3 tablespoons olive oil
12 slices bread or toasts (page 76)
Coarse salt
Strips of red pimiento, optional
Quince sauce (page 241), optional

Place the slices of pork loin in a nonreactive container. Sprinkle them with salt, pepper, oregano, pimentón, garlic, bay leaves, cloves and vinegar. Cover and refrigerate for 24 to 48 hours, turning the meat once or twice.

Remove the pork from the marinade, discarding the bay leaves and cloves. Heat the oil in a large, heavy frying pan. Fry the pork slices until browned, about 2 minutes per side. Remove and place on top of toast. Sprinkle with coarse salt. Place a few strips of red pimiento or a spoonful of quince sauce on top of the pork. Serve hot or room temperature.

Montadito de Morcilla
BLOOD SAUSAGE WITH RAISINS
AND PINE NUTS ON TOAST

Sweet raisins and crunchy pine nuts contrast with rich and spicy blood sausage. Serve these toasts alongside lentil soup for a hearty lunch. The sausage mixture is also good served with salad greens and a touch of Sherry vinegar.

Makes 10 tapas.

1 tablespoon olive oil
30 g / 1 oz / ¼ cup pine nuts
280 g / 10 oz *morcilla* (black pudding, blood sausage)
40 g / 1 ½ oz / ¼ cup seedless raisins
4 tablespoons white wine
10 toasts (page 76)

Heat the oil in a frying pan and fry the pine nuts until they are golden, about 30 seconds. Tilt the pan so the oil flows to one side and skim out the pine nuts.

Remove the casing and chop the sausage into small pieces. Add to the frying pan with the raisins and sauté on medium heat, breaking up the sausage pieces, 2 minutes. Add the wine and cook until sausage begins to sizzle again, 4 minutes.

Tilt the pan so fat flows to one side. Lift out the sausage with a slotted spoon and place it in a bowl. Divide the sausage mixture between the toasts, pressing it down. Sprinkle toasted pine nuts on top. Serve hot or room temperature.

Cojonudo
HAM AND EGGS ON TOAST

The name of this tapa, *cojonudo*, is rude slang for "fantastic" – a bit of hyperbole for such teensy eggs. To crack the quail eggs, give them a sharp tap with the blade of a knife, then break onto a saucer. Slip the egg from the saucer into hot oil in the frying pan. Fry four or five at a time. They cook in jiffy, so have the toast and ham waiting when you start the eggs.

Makes 10.

10 toasts (page 76)
2 tablespoons olive oil
100 g / 3 ½ oz thinly sliced serrano ham
10 quail eggs
2 piquillo peppers (from a tin)
Coarse salt
Hot pimentón (paprika) or cayenne

Place the toasts on a serving dish. Brush a frying pan with a little oil and heat it. Lay the slices of ham in the pan, turn them quickly and remove. Divide the ham between the toast.

Add remaining oil to the pan on medium heat. Break eggs, one at a time, into a saucer and slide them into the pan. Cook until whites are set but yolks still liquid, about 40 seconds. Lift the eggs out of the pan and place one on top of each toast.

Cut peppers into strips and lay one strip alongside each egg. Sprinkle with salt and pimentón. Serve immediately.

Paté de Sardinas
SARDINE PÂTÉ ON TOAST

A touch of Sherry and a jolt of lemon juice turn tinned sardines into a delightful pâté to spread on toast. The pâté keeps well, covered and refrigerated, so prepare it well in advance of a party.

Makes 20 to 22 tapas.

3 (120 g / 4 oz) tins sardines, drained
¼ large onion, chopped
1 teaspoon Dijon mustard
4 tablespoons lemon juice
2 tablespoons dry Sherry
3 tablespoons extra virgin olive oil
Salt and freshly ground black pepper
1 slice lemon, peeled and chopped
20 to 22 toasts (page 76)
2 hard-boiled eggs, sliced
Thin slices of peeled cucumber, to garnish
Parsley, to garnish

Combine the drained sardines, onion, mustard, lemon juice, Sherry, oil, salt and pepper in a blender or food processor. Blend to make a smooth spread. Stir the chopped lemon into it.

Shortly before serving, spread the sardine pâté on the toast. Place a slice of egg in the centre of each. Put half a slice of cucumber on either side of the egg. Place a parsley leaf on top of each egg.

Caballa Ahumada con Tostas
SMOKED MACKEREL ON TOAST

Capers cut the richness of smoked fish. Smoked trout could be used in place of the mackerel in this recipe.

Makes 10 tapas.

4 fillets of smoked mackerel (about 340 g / 12 oz)
1 spring onion, including some of the green, chopped
¼ teaspoon freshly ground black pepper
3 tablespoons drained capers
1 teaspoon grated lemon zest
4 tablespoons lemon juice
1 hard-boiled egg, chopped
3 tablespoons chopped parsley
10 toasts (page 76)
Salmon roe or other red "caviar", to garnish

Discard skin and any bones. Chop or shred the fish and place in a bowl. Add the onion, pepper, capers, lemon zest, juice, egg and parsley. Mix lightly with a fork.

Heap the mixture on toast, patting it down lightly. Garnish the tops with a scattering of red roe.

Tiznao
SALT COD AND ROASTED PEPPER ON TOAST

This tasty combo of cod and roasted vegetables can also be served in individual ramekins as a starter, with bread on the side for dipping. Flaked, tinned tuna is an alternative to the salt cod.

Makes 18 tapas or 6 starters.

350 g / 12 oz salt cod or drained, water-pack tuna
2 onions
2 red bell peppers
3 large tomatoes
1 head of garlic

3 tablespoons extra virgin olive oil
2 teaspoons pimentón (paprika)
Red chilli flakes
Salt and pepper
18 toasts (page 76)
Pitted and chopped olives, to garnish

Line a baking tin with foil and place the cod on it. Place under the grill (broiler) and grill until the surface of the cod is lightly toasted, 10 minutes. Turn the cod and grill until toasted, about 10 minutes. Discard liquid that accumulates in the pan. Remove the cod and place it in a bowl. Add water to cover and soak for 2 hours, changing the water twice. (If using tinned tuna, skip this step.)

Place the onions, peppers, tomatoes and garlic on the grill rack and roast them under the grill, turning occasionally, until the tomato skins split and the peppers and onions are charred. The tomatoes will take 10 minutes; the onions, garlic and peppers, about 25 minutes. Transfer the vegetables to a pan and cover with a lid.

When they are cool enough to handle,
peel the tomatoes, discard seeds and chop coarsely. Peel the peppers, discard seeds and stem and cut them into thin strips. Peel the onions and sliver them lengthwise. Slit open the garlic cloves and unwrap the softened garlic cloves. Cut them lengthwise.

Drain the soaked cod. With your fingers, separate it into flakes or crumbs, discarding all skin and bones.

Heat the oil in a frying pan. Add all the vegetables and cook over medium heat for 5 minutes. Cover and cook over low heat for 15 minutes. Stir in the cod (or tuna) flakes. Remove from heat and let stand, covered, for at least 30 minutes and up to 2 hours. Add salt to taste.

Immediately before serving, heap the cod and vegetables on toast. Scatter olives on top.

Brandada de Bacalao
GARLICKY SALT COD SPREAD ON TOAST

Start this recipe two or three days before you intend to serve it, as the salt cod needs to soak for 36 hours. (If you don't want to bother with the cod, try this spread with tinned tuna instead.) In La Mancha this spread is called *atascaburras* and it's served with chopped walnuts, but in Catalonia it's *brandada* and might be garnished with black olives. You can also serve the garlicky cod as a dip with breadsticks alongside.

Makes 20 to 22 tapas.

2 large potatoes (500 g / 1 lb 2 oz), peeled and cut in chunks
450 g / 1 lb salt cod, soaked in several changes of water for 36 hours
4 cloves garlic, crushed
120 ml / 4 fl oz / ½ cup extra virgin olive oil
Salt and pepper
20 to 22 toasts (page 76)
60 g / 2 oz / ½ cup coarsely chopped walnuts

Cook the potatoes in water to cover until almost tender, about 15 minutes. Lower the heat to a simmer and add the pieces of salt cod that have previously been soaked. Simmer, but do not boil, for 10 minutes. Lift the cod out with a slotted spoon and set aside to cool. Drain the potatoes, saving some of the liquid.

Mash the potatoes in a bowl with the crushed garlic. Stir in the oil, salt and pepper, and 6 to 8 spoonfuls of the reserved liquid to make a thick, smooth mash.

When cod is cool enough to handle, remove and discard all skin and bones. Shred or chop the cod and stir into the potatoes.

Shortly before serving, spoon mounds of the cod and potato mixture on toast. Sprinkle chopped walnuts on top. Serve at room temperature.

Mini de Sardinas Picantes
MINI ROLL WITH SPICY SARDINES

In the bars of el Tubo district, in the old quarter of Zaragoza, this tapa is known as a "*guardia civil.*" *Pimentón picante*, spicy-hot paprika, gives the sauce its fire power. If you haven't got this sort of pimentón, use cayenne, but in a lesser amount. *Piquillo* peppers, sweet and piquant, come tinned and ready to use. They are worth a search, but, if not available, use any tinned red pimiento. Buy small bread rolls (*bollos*) from bread shop or make the mini rolls (page 75).

Makes 12 mini rolls.

120 ml / 4 fl oz / ½ cup tinned tomato sauce or *tomate frito* (page 239)
1 tablespoon vinegar
2 teaspoons hot pimentón (paprika)
2 tablespoons finely chopped onion
60 g / 2 oz / ¼ cup chopped sweet pickles
12 mini rolls (page 75), split and toasted, if desired
6 tinned sardines, from 2 (120-g / 4-oz) tins, split
6 piquillo peppers, split, or tinned red pimiento, cut in strips

Combine the tomato sauce in a small bowl with the vinegar, pimentón, onion and chopped pickles. Spread a spoonful on the bottom half of each roll. Place half a sardine on each and top with half a piquillo pepper and cover with top of roll. Serve at room temperature.

Capote con Atún
MINI ROLL WITH TUNA

A *capote* is a cape, such as the big ones used to pass the bull in a bullfight. The "cape" of bright peppers covering the tuna makes for something far better than same-old tuna sandwiches. Wrap the sandwiches in cling film and take them along on your next picnic.

Short cut: Delicatessen counters at supermarkets often sell ready-roasted peppers.

Makes 8 mini rolls.

1 large green bell pepper
1 large red bell pepper
1 (266 g / 9 oz) tin light tuna, drained
1 tablespoon finely chopped spring onion
1 tablespoon drained capers
2 tablespoons lemon juice
Pinch of cayenne
120 ml / 4 fl oz / ½ cup mayonnaise
8 mini rolls (page 75)

Place the peppers on a pan and roast them under the grill (broiler), until charred on all sides, about 25 minutes total. Remove, cover the pan and allow to stand until cool. Peel the peppers and discard stem and seeds. Cut the peppers into wide strips.

Combine the tuna, onion, capers, lemon juice, cayenne and mayonnaise in a bowl.

Split the rolls in half. Spread tuna mixture on rolls. Top with strips of red and green peppers. Cover with top half of roll. Serve immediately or wrap each sandwich individually in plastic wrap and refrigerate up to 24 hours.

Escalivada
ROASTED AUBERGINES AND PEPPERS

Serve these roasted vegetables as a starter, rather like a salad; as a side dish with roasted meat, heaped on toast or as a topping for pizza. You can roast the aubergines and peppers under the grill (broiler) or over charcoal on the barbecue. If using for pizza, the vegetables can be prepared a day in advance and refrigerated, covered. Bring to room temperature before continuing with the recipe.

Serves 4 as a tapa or side dish. Use half the roasted aubergines and peppers as a topping for mini pizzas.

1 small aubergine (eggplant),
   about 285 g / 10 oz
1 red bell pepper, about 250 g / 8 ½ oz
1 medium onion
1 large tomato

1 small head garlic
1 teaspoon salt
Freshly ground black pepper
1 teaspoon vinegar
1 tablespoon olive oil

Arrange the aubergine, pepper, onion, and tomato in a shallow oven pan. Pierce the aubergine and pepper with a sharp knife in 3 or 4 places (to prevent steam from building up inside the skin). Slice the top off the head of garlic and add to the pan. Place the pan under the grill (broiler). Grill until aubergine and pepper are charred on one side, about 10 minutes. Use tongs to turn the vegetables. Return and grill until charred on all sides. Remove them to a bowl. (Peppers may need further turning to char all sides.)

Cover the vegetables and let them set until cool enough to handle. Peel the aubergine.

Chop or shred the flesh and place in a bowl. Peel and cut pepper in strips and add to the aubergine. Peel onion and cut in lengthwise slivers. Peel the tomato, discard juice and seeds and chop the flesh. Combine the vegetables and season them with salt and pepper

Squeeze the softened cloves of garlic from the skins into a small bowl. Mash them with a spoon. Stir the vinegar and oil into the garlic paste, then stir it into the vegetables.

Serve room temperature or use as topping for mini pizzas.

Menestra con Setas y Alcachofas
MUSHROOM AND ARTICHOKE MÉLANGE

Menestra can be made with all manner of seasonal vegetables—peas, carrots, asparagus. For this version, use two or more varieties of mushrooms to give the dish a complex, earthy flavour. Serve it heaped on toast as a tapa, as a starter, side dish or as a pizza topping.

Makes 6 to 8 tapas or side dishes or 4 starters. Use half of the mushroom and artichoke mélange as a topping for mini pizzas.

370 g / 13 oz mixed mushrooms
4 tablespoons olive oil
½ onion, sliced crosswise
2 cloves garlic, sliced crosswise
30 g / 1 oz chopped serrano ham
1 tomato, peeled, seeded and chopped
Salt and pepper
Pinch of thyme
1 (435 g / 15 oz) jar artichoke hearts, drained (about 230 g / 8 oz / 1 cup)

Clean the mushrooms carefully. Slice them crosswise.

Heat the oil in a frying pan and sauté the onion and garlic on medium heat for 5 minutes. Add the mushrooms and ham and continue sautéing on high heat until mushrooms release liquid and begin to brown. Add the tomato, salt, pepper, thyme and artichokes. Cook gently 15 minutes until most of the liquid has cooked away.

Serve hot or room temperature or use as topping for mini pizzas.

Coques
MINI PIZZAS WITH TWO TOPPINGS

Coques are the Catalan version of pizza – basic bread dough baked with different toppings. (Singular is *coca*.) While you can substitute prepared pizza bases, it's ever so easy to make them at home. Kids love punching dough – let them have a go.

Makes 14 (12 cm / 5 in) mini pizzas or 2 (30 cm / 12 in) pizzas.

To assemble the pizzas:
1 recipe Basic Bread Dough (page 74)
Olive oil to brush the pizzas
Roasted aubergine and peppers (use half of recipe page 69)
7 anchovy fillets from a tin
7 Arbequina olives
Oregano
Wild mushroom and artichoke mélange (use half of recipe page 70)
Shaved Manchego cheese

Preheat oven to 220ºC / 425ºF.

Divide the dough into 14 egg-sized balls (each about 50 g / 1 ¾ oz). Press or roll them into approximately 12-cm / 5-in rounds. (If making full-size pizzas, divide the dough in half and roll each half to 30-cm / 12-in circles.) Place the rounds on baking sheets that have been sprinkled with flour. Brush the dough with oil.

Spread half of the pizzas with the roasted aubergine and peppers. Place an olive in the centre of each. Cut an anchovy fillet in half and lay each strip next to the olive. Sprinkle with oregano.

Spread remaining pizza rounds with wild mushroom and artichoke mélange. Sprinkle with shaved cheese.

Bake the pizzas until edges are lightly browned, 15 minutes. Serve hot or room temperature.

Empanada de Bonito
EMPANADA WITH TUNA FILLING

Empanada is a robust pie with a bread crust and a savoury filling. It makes great snack food. Tinned tuna is an easy and tasty filling, but you can vary the filling to suit your tastes. Try shellfish such as clams, mussels or scallops; thinly sliced and fried pork loin; sardines, or cooked chicken breast in place of the tuna.

Bake the empanada on a pizza stone or on a large oven tin. A 35-cm / 13 ½-in paella pan works just fine.

Makes 12 servings.

1 recipe for Basic Bread Dough (page 74)
5 tablespoons olive oil
2 large onions (450 g / 1 lb), chopped
2 green bell peppers (450 g / 1 lb), chopped
4 cloves garlic, chopped
60 g / 2 oz chorizo sausage, chopped
30 g / 1 oz serrano ham, chopped
2 tablespoons chopped parsley
Pinch of oregano

2 teaspoons sweet pimentón (paprika)
Pinch of cayenne
2 tablespoons water
Salt and freshly ground black pepper
Flour to roll out the dough
Maize or wheat flour for the pan
400 g / 14 oz tinned white tuna, drained
1 (80-g / 2 ¾-oz) tin red pimiento, drained
1 egg, beaten (you won't need all of it)

While the dough is rising, prepare the filling. Heat the oil in a large frying pan on medium heat and sauté the onions, peppers and garlic 5 minutes. Add the chorizo, ham, parsley and oregano and cook, uncovered, until onions are very soft, 15 minutes. Remove from heat. In a small bowl, stir the pimentón and cayenne into the water until smooth. Stir it into the onion mixture. Season with salt and pepper.

Preheat oven to 220ºC / 425ºF.

Punch down the dough and turn it out onto a lightly floured board. Knead in 1 tablespoon olive oil, as directed in the dough recipe. Divide the dough in half.

Roll and stretch one piece of dough to a 35-cm / 13 ½-in circle. Fit it into a shallow oven tin that has been dusted lightly with maize or wheat flour. Spread the onion mixture on the dough.

Break the tuna into chunks and layer it on top of the onion mixture. Cut the pimiento into strips and lay it on top of the tuna. Roll out remaining piece of dough and place on top of the filling. Roll and twist the edges of the dough together. Trim off any excess dough.

Use trimmings to roll long cords to decorate the top of the empanada. Cut two slits in the top for steam to escape. Brush the top with beaten egg.

Bake the empanada until golden-brown on top, 30 minutes.

Serve hot or room temperature.

VARIATION
Like a jolt of hot chilli? Sprinkle chopped *guindillas*, pickled green chillies from a jar, on top of the tuna chunks along with the red pimiento.

BASIC BREAD DOUGH

This basic bread dough can be used for the empanada and pizza crusts or for making bread rolls. The basic dough can be prepared in advance of baking. After it has risen, wrap tightly in plastic wrap and refrigerate up to two days or freeze for two weeks. Thaw completely before rolling out the dough.

2 teaspoons active dry yeast (6 g / ¼ oz)
1 teaspoon sugar
250 ml / 9 fl oz / 1 cup +1 tablespoon very warm water (38º-43ºC / 100º-110ºF), divided
450 g / 1 lb / 4 cups +2 tablespoons plain flour plus additional for dusting baking sheets
1 teaspoon salt
3 tablespoons olive oil plus additional for the bowl

Place the yeast and sugar in a small bowl and add 6 tablespoons of the warm water. Stir to dissolve. Allow it to stand 5 minutes until bubbly.

Combine the flour and salt in a large bowl. Make a well in the centre and add the yeast mixture, remaining warm water and 2 tablespoons of the oil. Stir to combine the ingredients into a ball. Turn out on a board and knead the dough until smooth and glossy, 5 minutes. If dough is very sticky, sprinkle it with a little flour. It will gradually become less sticky with kneading.

Clean out the mixing bowl and oil it lightly. Gather the dough into a ball and turn it in the bowl to coat on all sides with oil. Cover with a dampened cloth and leave in a warm place to rise until doubled in bulk, one to two hours.

Punch down the dough and turn it out onto the board. Press the dough out flat and sprinkle it with the remaining 1 tablespoon of oil. Fold the dough over several times, then knead until the oil is incorporated.

Bollitos y Molletes
MINI ROLLS AND MAXI ROLLS

Use these rolls – mini or maxi – for the toasts and sandwiches in this chapter. They're delicious when fresh-baked but every bit as good when toasted lightly. The molletes make fine hamburger buns as well.

Makes 20 mini rolls or 10 maxi rolls.

1 recipe for Basic Bread Dough (page 74)
Flour for dusting baking sheet

After the dough has risen once, punch it down and turn out onto a board. Pat the dough out flat and sprinkle it with the remaining tablespoon of oil, as directed in the recipe. Fold the dough and knead until oil is incorporated.

To make mini rolls, divide the dough into 20 small balls, each approximately 35 g / 1 ¼ oz. Flatten them slightly and place 5 cm / 2 in apart on baking sheets that have been lightly dusted with flour.

For maxi rolls, divide dough into 10 balls, each approximately 70 g / 2 ½ oz. Pat them as flat as possible and place 5 cm / 2 in apart on baking sheets.

Cover with a dry cloth and allow to rise for 30 minutes.

Preheat oven to 220ºC / 425ºF.

Bake the rolls until golden on top, about 20 minutes. Cool them completely before storing in air-tight bags.

Tostas y Tostadas
TOASTS

These crispy toasts make a good base for savoury spreads and tapa toppings. They keep well in an air-tight container, so you can prepare them in advance of a party. Don't add the toppings until shortly before serving. The number of toasts from a loaf will depend on the shape and weight of the bread. Skinny baguettes will yield more, but smaller, slices than the standard *barra* (a long loaf that is wider and thicker than baguette) called for in this recipe.

Makes 20 to 22 toasts.

300 g / 10 ½ oz long loaf of bread
4 tablespoons olive oil

Preheat oven to 190ºC / 375ºF.

Slice the bread on the diagonal, 15 mm / ½ in thick. Lay the slices on a baking sheet and brush the tops with oil. Bake 6 minutes. Reverse position of baking sheet and bake until lightly golden, 6 minutes more.

Cool on racks. Store in air-tight bags or tins.

Regañás
WHEAT CRISPS

These crispy crackers, popular at tapa bars in Sevilla and Cádiz, are seriously addictive! They're good all by themselves or as dippers for sauces. They keep well stored in an air-tight container, so make a big batch of them and bring them out at your next drinks party.

Makes about 250 crisps.

1 teaspoon active dry yeast (3 g / ⅛ oz)
½ teaspoon sugar
250 ml / 9 fl oz / 1 cup+1 tablespoon very warm water
200 g / 7 oz / 1 ¾ cup whole wheat flour
250 g / 8 ¾ oz / 2 ⅓ cup plain flour plus additional for rolling out dough
2 teaspoons salt
30 g / 1 oz / 3 tablespoons sesame seeds
2 tablespoons olive oil plus additional to oil bowl

Combine the yeast and sugar in a small bowl. Add 4 tablespoons of the warm water and stir to dissolve. Allow to stand until bubbly.

Combine the two kinds of flour in a bowl with the salt and sesame seeds. Make a well in the centre and add the yeast, oil and remaining warm water. Stir to mix the dry ingredients with the wet.

Turn out on a board and knead the dough. It will be rough and shaggy at first and gradually become smooth and glossy. Clean out the mixing bowl and oil it lightly. Gather the dough into a ball and turn it in the bowl to coat with oil. Cover with a damp cloth and place in a warm place until doubled in bulk, about two hours.

Preheat oven to 220ºC / 425ºF.

Punch down the dough. Divide it in four pieces. Place one piece on a lightly floured board. Roll it out as thinly as possible into a roughly rectangular shape. With a sharp knife or kitchen scissors, cut the dough into strips 25 mm / 1 in wide. Cut the strips crosswise into 5-cm /2-in pieces. Place them on a baking sheet. Repeat with remaining dough.

Bake the strips until browned on the edges, about 10 minutes.

Allow to cool before storing in an air-tight container.

Pintxos

SMALL BITES

Pintxos
SMALL BITES

Figs with Ham (*Higos con Jamón*)

Quince Paste with Cheese (*Membrillo con Queso*)

Blood Sausage with Apple (*Morcilla con Manzana*)

Olive, Anchovy and Pickled Pepper Bites (*Gilda*)

Mussel, Quail Egg and Cherry Tomato Bites (*Pintxo de Mejillones en Escabeche*)

Salt Cod in Garlic Pil Pil Sauce (*Bacalao al Pil Pil*)

Salt Cod How-To

Beetroot, Cheese and Sausage Bites (*Pintxo de Remolacha y Queso*)

Octopus and Potatoes, Galician Style (*Pulpo y Cachelos a la Gallega*)

Stuffed Mushrooms (*Champiñones Rellenos*)

Beef Fillet Tips with Sherry (*Punta de Solomillo*)

Olive Picks

If you can stick it on a pick and eat it in one or two bites, what you have is a *pintxo*, which is the Basque spelling for *pincho*, meaning something skewered on a cocktail stick. In the Basque Country of northern Spain, *pintxos* are the equivalent of tapas. *Ir de pintxos* is to go tapa-hopping from bar to bar, sampling the specialties of each.

The simplest pintxos, sometimes known as *banderillas*, or "barbs," are just a selection of pickled foods right out of the jar or tin, such as olives, gherkins, pickled onions, often combined with cheese, tuna, ham and hard-boiled egg. The salty-sour flavours prickle the taste buds. Contrasts in texture and taste tease the appetite.

But Basque pintxos are often much more elaborate. Sometimes called *alta cocina en miniatura*—haute cuisine in miniature —they include totally traditional dishes, such as salt cod in garlic pil pil sauce, or wildly innovative ones, such as sea urchin foam and anchovy ravioli or cod served atop twigs of smoking rosemary. Served in bite-sized portions, sometimes with a supporting base of bread, and held together with a cocktail stick, these are truly one-bite gastronomy.

Pintxos make great party food. Most can be prepared well in advance. Besides the recipes that follow, here are some other ideas for what to stick on a pick. Think: contrast in colour and taste. Go a little crazy. Open up all those tins of gourmet Spanish food and mix and match them. See Sauces, Dressings, Dips and Spreads for recipes for sauces to accompany the pintxos. See Olive Picks (page 92) for more about this favourite garnish.

Prawn, olive, tuna and a dollop of mayonnaise.

Asparagus tip (tinned), ham and twist of piquillo pepper.

Prawn, egg and artichoke with *alioli* (garlic mayonnaise).

Artichoke heart (tinned), ham and *romesco*, Catalan red pepper sauce.

Tuna, pickle and anchovy with vinaigrette.

Caper berry, onion and anchovy.

Green chillies, anchovies and piquillo peppers with cheese.

Chorizo sausage with cheese and piquillo peppers.

Green olives, black olives and anchovies.

Smoked salmon with *gulas* (fake elvers).

Maridajes–Salado y Dulce
PAIRINGS–SALTY AND SWEET

Here is a trio of easy-to-prepare appetisers. Their allure comes from contrasts in flavour—salty and sweet—and textures—crisp and smooth. They go equally well with dry Sherry or cocktails and would be the perfect hors d'oeuvres to pass to guests before a dinner party.

Higos con Jamón
FIGS WITH HAM

In the late summer, you can prepare these appetisers using fresh, ripe figs in place of dry ones. Peel the fresh figs, cut them in half and skewer on cocktail sticks with ham.

Makes 10 tapas.

10 small dry figs (about 90 g / 3 oz)
1 tablespoon dry Sherry
4 tablespoons boiling water
90 g / 3 oz thinly sliced serrano ham

Wash figs in running water. Remove stems and, if the figs are large, cut them in half. Place them in a small bowl. Add the Sherry and boiling water and allow to stand 10 minutes. Drain.

Stick the figs on cocktail sticks. Trim ham of excess fat and tough ends. Cut into about 10 strips. Roll up a strip and fasten it onto a cocktail stick with a fig. Place on serving platter.

Membrillo con Queso
QUINCE PASTE WITH CHEESE

Dulce de membrillo is sweet quince paste, a jam that sets up firm in a rectangular mould. Buy it, sliced to order, at the cheese counter or, packaged, with other fruit preserves. Here, it's paired with aged Manchego, but for breakfast or dessert, serve it with mild, fresh cheese.

Makes 10 tapas.

100 g / 3 ½ oz aged Manchego cheese
1 (12-mm / ½-in thick) slab of quince paste (about 140 g / 5 oz)

Cut cheese into 10 (25-mm / 1-in) cubes. Cut quince paste into 10 cubes.

Skewer first quince then cheese on 10 cocktail sticks.

Morcilla con Manzana
BLOOD SAUSAGE WITH APPLE

You could use any variety of morcilla, black pudding (blood sausage), for this sausage-apple combo.

Makes 10 tapas.

85 g / 3 oz blood sausage
1 Granny Smith apple

Cut the sausage into 10 (10-mm / ⅜-in) slices and remove casing. Peel and core the apple and cut it into 10 thin slices. Skewer a slice of sausage crosswise on a cocktail stick and stick it upright into an apple slice. Arrange on a serving dish.

Gilda
OLIVE, ANCHOVY AND PICKLED PEPPER BITES

In San Sebastian, in the Basque Country, the Gilda is the primordial pintxo, supposedly invented in the early 1950s to immortalize Rita Hayworth in the film of the same name—Hayworth being "hot", "salty," "smooth," and "green" (?). Go figure. Nowadays, the gastronomical equivalent of an Oscar is called the *Gilda de Oro*, the "golden Gilda", awarded for the best pintxo. Skinny pickled green chilli peppers—*guindillas*—are mild, like Italian *peperoncini*. They come in jars, ready to use. Layer them on your next tuna sandwich too.

Makes 10 tapas.

10 pickled green chilli peppers
10 fillets of tinned anchovies, drained
10 pitted green olives
Extra virgin olive oil

Trim off stems from green chillies. Skewer
a chilli on a cocktail stick with an anchovy
folded in half and an olive. Place on a serving
dish. When all of the bites are prepared,
drizzle them with oil. Serve room temperature.

Pintxo de Mejillones en Escabeche
MUSSEL, QUAIL EGG AND CHERRY TOMATO BITES

Mussels tinned in an escabeche marinade are quick. You could also use fresh mussels, steamed open in wine, or cooked prawns (shrimp) for this appetiser.

Makes 20 tapas.

10 quail eggs
1 (112-g / 4-oz) tin small mussels in escabeche, drained
10 cherry tomatoes, halved

Hard-boil the eggs, 4 minutes. Plunge them into cold water. Peel them when cool and cut them in half.

Spear on a cocktail stick: a mussel, half an egg and half a tomato, cut-side down. Stand them upright on a serving dish. Serve cold or room temperature.

Bacalao al Pil Pil
SALT COD IN GARLIC PIL PIL SAUCE

If you've ever gone pinxto-hopping in Bilbao's Old Quarter, in the neighbourhood surrounding Plaza Nueva, probably you savoured this emblematic Basque dish—salt cod with a thick, golden garlic sauce. Much mystique accompanies pil pil, which consists of nothing more than cod, olive oil and garlic. First you have to convert the stiff, cardboard-like dry cod into white, flaky fish. Then you have to magically thicken the olive oil into an unctuous and delicious sauce, by slowly swirling the warmed oil into the cod. The gelatine in its skin combines with the oil to make a sauce as thick as mayonnaise. The clever Basques even invented an electric device that keeps the cazuela rocking, freeing up hands for other jobs.

A cazuela—earthenware casserole—is perfect for cooking this dish because it holds the heat. You can use a frying pan instead, but take care never to let the cod cook too hot.

■ SALT COD HOW-TO

Shops that specialise in salt cod products sell centre-cut "loins" of cod, already free of bones. This will save you time. But if you are starting out with a whole cod, here's how to proceed. Cut off the top quarter and bottom (tail) lengths and save them for another use (see Salt Cod in the index for some ideas). Cut the centre (about 700 g / 1 ½ lb) into four equal pieces. Wash the cod, place it in a nonreactive bowl and cover with water. Cover the bowl and refrigerate. Soak the cod 36 hours,

changing the water 4 times a day.

Drain the cod and squeeze out excess water. Use a filleting knife to remove all fins, bones and scales from the cod, but leave the skin intact. Cut away (and save for another use) any thin-fleshed and bony sections. The soaked and trimmed cod will weigh 500 to 600 g / 1 lb 2 oz to 1 lb 5 oz. If it is to be served as tapas, cut the pieces into about 12 equal-sized cubes. Pat them dry on paper towels.

Makes 12 tapas or 4 main courses.

700 g / 1 ½ lb centre-cut salt cod with skin, soaked and filleted (see how-to, left)
375 ml / 13 fl oz / 1 ½ cups extra virgin olive oil
4 cloves garlic, sliced crosswise
1 or more small dry red chillies, sliced crosswise
12 thin slices bread, crusts removed, to serve

If the cod is to be served as tapas, cut it into 12 (5-cm / 2-in) cubes.

Heat the oil in a 25-cm / 10-in cazuela (earthenware casserole) or frying pan. Add the sliced garlic and chillies and fry until garlic is just golden, 30 seconds. Remove the cazuela from the heat and skim out the garlic and chillies and reserve them.

Place the pieces of cod in the oil and cook on a low heat for 5 minutes. Don't fry the cod. Do not let the oil bubble. Lift the cod out of the oil onto a plate. Carefully pour the oil in the cazuela into a heat-proof jug (measuring cup).

Return the cod to the cazuela, skin side up. Add 2 tablespoons of the warm oil. Place the cazuela on a board or counter top and gently swirl the oil and cod in a circular motion. When the oil begins to thicken, add 1 tablespoon more warm oil. Swirl the cazuela until the oil emulsifies, then add another spoonful of oil. Continue adding oil, a spoonful at a time, rocking and swirling the cazuela, until all the oil is incorporated and sauce is as thick as mayonnaise. Be patient— this will take about 15 minutes.

The sauce will hold at room temperature for up to an hour. To reheat, place the cazuela on a very low heat. Stir the sauce as it warms. Do not overheat or the sauce will separate.

To serve, place pieces of cod, skin side down, on the sliced bread. Spoon the sauce on top. Top with sliced garlic and chilli. Stick with cocktail sticks and serve warm or room temperature.

Pintxo de Remolacha y Queso
BEETROOT, CHEESE AND SAUSAGE BITES

Salchichón is a peppery, dry-cure sausage, somewhat like salami. It makes a tasty contrast with bland white goat cheese (*queso fresco de cabra*) and chunks of marinated beetroot (beets).

Makes 20 tapas.

140 g / 5 oz cooked beetroot (beets), (2 medium)
1 tablespoon extra virgin olive oil
1 tablespoon wine vinegar
Salt and pepper
140 g / 5 oz fresh white goat cheese
85 g / 3 oz salchichón

Cut the beetroot into 20 (25 mm / 1 in) cubes. Place in a bowl and add oil, vinegar, salt and pepper. Marinate at least 1 hour and up to 24.

Cut cheese into 25-mm / 1-in cubes. Cut salchichón into about 20 pieces.

On each cocktail stick, spear first a piece of beetroot, then cheese and finally salchichón. Serve at room temperature.

Pulpo y Cachelos a la Gallega
OCTOPUS AND POTATOES, GALICIAN STYLE

This is an easy pintxo to prepare if you can buy pre-cooked, cut-up octopus. In Galicia it is served on wooden plates, the octopus and potatoes (called *cachelos*) dribbled with *ajada*, a simple sauce of garlic, pimentón and olive oil. Do serve this on individual plates, as the sauce is a little too messy to be passed around.

Makes about 25 tapas.

3 medium potatoes (350 g / ¾ lb)
1 tablespoon pimentón (paprika)
¼ teaspoon cayenne
2 cloves garlic, crushed
½ teaspoon salt
90 ml / 3 fl oz / ⅓ cup extra virgin olive oil
1 teaspoon vinegar
500 g / 1 lb 2 oz cooked and cut-up octopus
Coarse salt, to serve

Cook the unpeeled potatoes in boiling water until just tender, 15 to 20 minutes. Drain. When cool, peel the potatoes, cut them in half lengthwise, then crosswise into slices about 12 mm / ½ in thick.

In a small bowl combine the pimentón, cayenne, garlic, salt, oil and vinegar.

Plunge the cut-up octopus into boiling water and drain immediately. Stick 2 or 3 pieces of octopus on each cocktail stick and stick it into a potato slice. Place on a dish. Stir the dressing and spoon it over the octopus and potatoes. Sprinkle with coarse salt. Serve room temperature.

Champiñones Rellenos
STUFFED MUSHROOMS

The Basques, who have their own language, use a disconcerting mix of consonants. Thus, *txampis*, short for *champiñones*, mushrooms. A whiff of brandy gives added depth of flavour to these stuffed mushrooms, always a favourite at drinks parties. Serve them, too, for breakfast or brunch.

Makes 12 tapas.

12 large white mushrooms with stems
   (about 450 g / 1 lb)
3 tablespoons olive oil
4 tablespoons finely chopped onion
4 tablespoons finely chopped green pepper
1 clove chopped garlic

2 tablespoons finely chopped serrano ham
Salt and pepper
Pinch of thyme
1 tablespoon brandy
12 toasts (page 76), crusts removed

Clean the mushrooms, cut off stems and, with a small spoon, hollow out the caps, saving the trimmings. Finely chop the stems and trimmings and reserve.

Heat 2 tablespoons of the oil in a large frying pan. Sauté the onion, green pepper and garlic on medium heat for 5 minutes. Add the ham and chopped mushroom stems and sauté 5 minutes more. Season with salt, pepper, thyme and brandy. Cook 5 minutes and remove from heat. Place the filling mixture in a bowl.

Add the remaining 1 tablespoon oil to the pan. Place the mushroom caps, stem side down, in the oil and let brown 4 minutes. Turn the caps and brown the bottoms, 4 minutes. Mushroom juices will collect in the caps. Carefully transfer the caps to a plate without spilling the juices. Spoon the filling into the caps. Place each one on a square of toast and stick with a wooden cocktail stick. Serve hot or room temperature.

Mushrooms can be reheated before serving. Place cocktail sticks with mushrooms and toasts on an oven tin and heat in a hot oven for 3 minutes.

Punta de Solomillo
BEEF FILLET TIPS WITH SHERRY

This is a ravishingly good tapa, a Sevilla favourite—succulent bites of fillet steak (tenderloin), quickly sautéed with garlic and Sherry. The tapa originated when some butcher unloaded those skinny tips of the fillet, too thin to cut as a steak, at a good price to a tapa cook, who recognized a bargain. So popular is the tapa nowadays, that the "tip" is cut from the centre fillet. You could accompany it with onion sauce (page 146) or Cabrales cheese sauce (page 240), but it really doesn't need anything.

Makes 10 tapas.

2 (25-mm / 1-in thick) slices beef fillet steak (tenderloin), about 200 g / 7 oz
Salt and freshly ground black pepper
2 cloves garlic, slivered lengthwise
2 tablespoons olive oil
60 ml / 2 fl oz / ¼ cup dry Sherry
5 toasts (page 76), cut in half
Coarse salt

Flatten the slices of fillet steak slightly. Cut each into 5 cubes. Sprinkle them with salt and pepper and slivered garlic. Allow to stand at room temperature 30 to 40 minutes.

Heat the oil in a small frying pan. On high heat, add the beef and garlic and sauté until browned on all sides, about 2 minutes. Skim the meat out and keep warm. Add the Sherry to the pan. Reduce on high heat for 1 minute. Pour the juices over the pieces of beef.

Set a piece of beef on each toast and skewer with a cocktail stick. Drizzle the pan juices over the meat. Sprinkle with coarse salt. Serve hot or room temperature.

■ OLIVE PICKS

The waiter serves your *copas* of fino Sherry and sets a little dish of olives on the table. You nibble the olives, sip the Sherry, chat with friends. This is, surely, the quintessential tapas experience; olives the quintessential tapa. A little tangy, a little salty, they are the perfect accompaniment to wine. And, Spain is olive country.

If you have ever, innocently, plucked an olive right off the tree and popped it into your mouth, you were probably shocked at that taste—bitter, astringent and altogether inedible. Olives need processing to turn them into tapa treats.

How table olives are processed, or cured, is one way of categorising them. The other is by olive varietal. Process and variety make for a wondrous range of types of eating olives.

The most familiar olives, known world-wide, are bottled or tinned Manzanilla olives, often marketed as "Sevilla" olives. Manzanilla is the name of the variety of olive tree. It produces a plump, meaty olive. Manzanillas make up the bulk of the table olive production, but the fat Gordal olive (also called "queen") is another favourite commercial table olive. Both varieties have a good proportion of flesh to pit. They are hand-picked when still green. The curing process entails first soaking in an alkaline solution to remove the bitterness. Then the olives are left in a brine to ferment, which converts the olives' natural sugars into lactic acid. This is what gives them that wonderful tangy flavour.

Manzanilla olives may additionally be pitted and stuffed—with strips of red pimiento, with anchovy paste, with almonds and, in some of the newer market versions, even with smoked salmon.

Most olive varieties, when fully ripe, turn a purplish colour, not black. Black olives that you buy in a tin—gorgeous for garnishing salads and cold dishes—are not really ripe olives. They also are picked green, processed in alkaline solution, then the black colour is fixed by oxidation.

But these are by no means the only Spanish olives you will find in tapa bars. Every olive-producing region has its particular varieties and methods of curing and flavouring olives. Rarely are these exported. They are seasonal produce, with no long shelf life. Here are some to try.

In Andalusian bars, you might sample *aceitunas partidas*, green olives (Manzanilla, Hojiblanca or Morisco) that have been cracked to split them open, then brine-cured (no alkaline is used). They may be flavoured with thyme, fennel, cloves of garlic, slices of lemon, oregano and strips of red pepper. In Extremadura and La Mancha, ripe Cornicabra and Cacereña olives are prepared *rayado*, incised with a sharp blade, then cured

If you have ever, innocently, plucked an olive right off the tree and popped it into your mouth, you were probably shocked at that taste – bitter, astringent and altogether inedible.

in brine and flavoured with local herbs. Arbequina is the varietal best-known in Catalonia, especially Lérida. These are tiny olives with a delicate flavour, simply brine-cured. The Empeltre olives of Aragón and Navarra are cured in brine when they reach a purplish-black degree of ripeness. In Murcia and Alicante, the Cuquillo olive is cured when nearly black.

While any of these olives make great tapas, they also are incorporated in salads, cooked dishes and sauces. Olive paste or pâté, called *olivada* (page 246), makes a wonderful sandwich spread.

You can add flavour to bottled, store-bought olives by draining them, then marinating for two days in salt water with slivered garlic, fresh or dried thyme, a sliced lemon and a splash of extra virgin olive oil.

Platos Fríos

SALADS & COLD DISHES

Platos Fríos
SALADS AND COLD DISHES

Cauliflower Salad with Olives (*Ensalada de Coliflor con Aceitunas*)

Málaga Salad with Oranges and Olives (*Ensalada Malagueña*)

Fresh Tomato and Pepper Salad (*Pipirrana*)

Potato Salad with Lemon Dressing (*Papas Aliñadas*)

"Russian" Potato Salad (*Ensaladilla Rusa*)

Shellfish Cocktail (*Salpicón de Mariscos*)

Marinated Artichokes with Catalan Sausage (*Alcachofas con Romesco y Butifarra*)

Chickpea Salad with Sausage (*Garbanzos Aliñados*)

Roasted Pepper Salad (*Ensalada de Pimientos Asados*)

Stuffed Eggs with Prawns (*Huevos Rellenos con Gambas*)

Marinated Fresh Anchovies (*Boquerones en Vinagre*)

Mussels Vinaigrette (*Mejillones a la Vinagreta*)

Fish in Escabeche Marinade (*Caballa en Escabeche*)

Lollipops of Quail in Escabeche Marinade (*ChupaChups de Codorniz en Escabeche*)

Gazpacho in a Glass (*Gazpacho en Vasito*)

White Gazpacho Shooters with Grapes (*Ajo Blanco con Uvas en Copitas*)

Cooked Prawns (*Gambas Cocidas, Langostinos Cocidos*)

platos fríos
SALADS AND COLD DISHES

Check out the dishes lined up on the bar. Stuffed eggs napped in mayonnaise. Piquant seafood cocktail. Roasted peppers bathed in olive oil. Runner beans with a garlic dressing. A heaping platter of cooked prawns. A glance down the bar shows you that salads and other prepared cold dishes make up the biggest variety of a tapa bar's daily offerings. A bar on a typical day might have as many as a dozen different cold dishes!

Salads and cold tapas are especially adaptable to home entertaining. For a buffet supper, choose several of them and add a main dish of meat, poultry or fish to complete the menu. Many of these salads make superb side dishes, to accompany a summer barbecue meal.

Most tapa salads start with a stop at the produce market, but a few can be conjured up from ingredients in the pantry. Interesting sauces will turn simple cooked veggies into extra special tapas. Some examples: boiled potatoes with *alioli*, garlic mayonnaise; shredded cabbage with *romesco*, Catalan red pepper sauce, or lettuce hearts with Cabrales blue cheese sauce. (Find these recipes in Sauces, Dressings, Dips and Spreads.)

Shellfish is a very special category amongst cold dishes on the tapa bar. A few establishments might have a raw bar, serving oysters or *conchas finas*, big clams, opened to order. But most serve cooked shellfish, still in their shells. Here are some of the best. *Cigalas* are huge prawns with claws like miniature lobsters (also known as Norway lobsters, Dublin Bay prawns or sea crayfish). Fresh ones are sublime. Frozen are not so good. Prawns (shrimp) come in several sizes and nomenclature. Big ones are *langostinos*, while medium-sized ones are *gambas*. Wee ones are *camarones*. *Carabineros* are enormous, dark red prawns. Spain has some prawns famed for their sweet flavour—the *langostinos* of Sanlúcar de Barrameda, Viñaroz, San Carlos de Rápita, and Santa Pola. If you find these, they will cost a lot.

While mussels and clams are usually cooked to order, shellfish such as prawns, winkles, sea snails and small crabs are precooked and served cold. Typically, cold shellfish is accompanied by nothing more complicated than lemon wedges.

In fishing ports, such as El Puerto de Santa María (Cádiz), you select your cooked shellfish at a *cocedero*, where it is weighed and dished into a paper cone. Then you carry it around the corner to a bar, where you order the accompanying fino or white wine.

Ensalada de Coliflor con Aceitunas
CAULIFLOWER SALAD WITH OLIVES

Here's a simple dressing—olive oil, garlic, paprika and vinegar—that works with lots of different vegetables, whether served hot or cold. Use it with green beans, broccoli, asparagus, potatoes, as well as cauliflower.

Makes 10 tapas or side dishes.

1 small cauliflower (900 g / 2 lb)
4 tablespoons olive oil
4 cloves garlic, sliced crosswise
1 small dry red chilli, sliced crosswise
1 teaspoon pimentón (paprika)
Pinch of fennel seed (optional)
1 teaspoon salt
3 tablespoons vinegar
2 tablespoons water
60 g / 2 oz pitted, brine-cured green olives
4 tablespoons chopped flat-leaf parsley

Cut the cauliflower into florets, discarding thick stems. Bring a large pan of salted water to the boil and cook the cauliflower until crisp-tender, about 4 minutes after water returns to the boil. Drain and refresh in cold water.

Heat the oil in a frying pan and sauté the garlic and chilli 20 seconds. Remove the pan from the heat and stir in the pimentón, fennel seed, salt and vinegar. Add the water to make a smooth dressing. Stir it into the cauliflower. Allow to marinate at room temperature for 1 hour.

Ensalada Malagueña
MÁLAGA SALAD WITH ORANGES AND OLIVES

This exotic Málaga salad is traditionally made with bacalao, salt cod that is first toasted, then shredded. The combination of oranges, olive oil and olives also works very well with substitutions for the cod, such as tinned tuna, cooked prawns or thinly sliced serrano ham. Try this salad as a starter for a holiday dinner.

Makes 12 tapas or 6 starters.

Salad greens (optional)
4 oranges, peeled and pith removed
1 small red onion or 6 scallions, thinly sliced
10 green or black pitted olives
1 clove garlic, finely chopped
2 tablespoons extra virgin olive oil
1 tablespoon Sherry vinegar
Pinch of red chilli flakes
180 g / 6 oz drained tuna, shredded cod, peeled prawns or slivered ham

Arrange salad greens on serving platter or individual plates.

Slice the oranges and cut into bite-sized pieces. Arrange them on the greens. Scatter the onions on top. Arrange the olives on the oranges.

In a small bowl, combine the garlic, oil, vinegar and chilli.

Scatter the tuna, cod, prawns or ham on top of the oranges. Drizzle with the dressing. Allow to stand 30 minutes before serving.

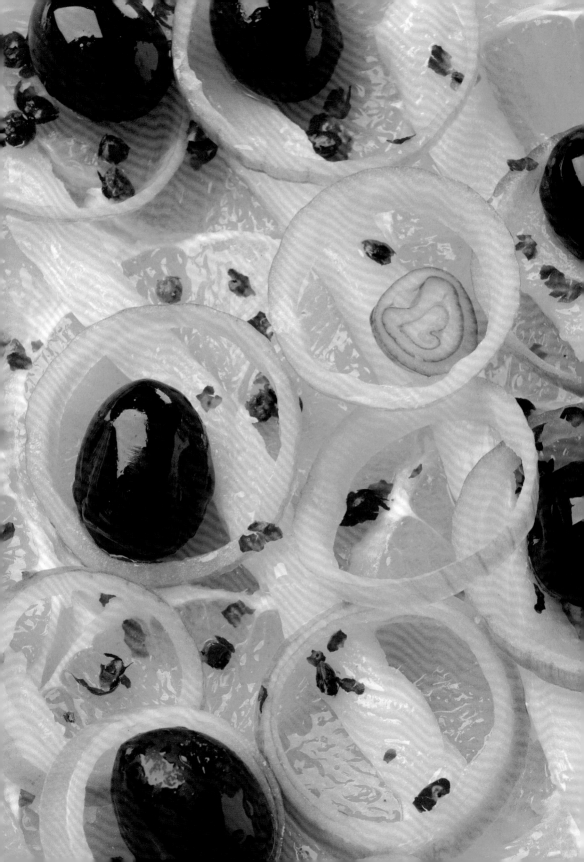

Pipirrana
FRESH TOMATO AND PEPPER SALAD

Here's a favourite tapa dish in southern Spain—usually garnished with tuna, but sometimes with strips of serrano ham.

Makes 18 tapas or 6 starters.

6 medium-sized ripe tomatoes, chopped
3 spring onions or 1 small onion, chopped
2 green bell peppers, finely chopped
1 small cucumber, peeled and chopped
1 clove garlic, finely chopped
1 teaspoon salt
2 tablespoons chopped flat-leaf parsley
3 tablespoons wine vinegar
6 tablespoons extra virgin olive oil
1 (90-g / 3-oz) tin tuna, drained
1 hard-boiled egg, chopped

Combine the tomatoes, onions, peppers, cucumber and garlic in a bowl. Add the salt and parsley. Drizzle with the vinegar and oil and toss the salad gently. Arrange it on a platter. Garnish the top with chunks of tuna and chopped egg. Serve cold or room temperature.

Papas Aliñadas
POTATO SALAD WITH LEMON DRESSING

This is a favourite tapa throughout Andalusia. It makes a great side dish with summertime barbecue foods too.

Makes 10 to 12 tapas or 6 side dishes.

5 to 6 medium potatoes (900 g / 2 lb)
1 teaspoon salt
4 spring onions, finely chopped
2 medium tomatoes, chopped
4 tablespoons extra virgin olive oil
6 tablespoons fresh lemon juice
2 tablespoons chopped flat-leaf parsley
2 hard-boiled eggs, sliced, for garnish
1 (90 g / 3 oz) tin tuna, drained, for garnish
Strips of tinned red pimiento, for garnish
12 pitted green olives, for garnish

Cook the potatoes in their skins in boiling water until just tender, 20 minutes. Drain. When cool, peel and slice the potatoes.

In a large bowl, combine the salt, onions, tomatoes, oil, lemon juice and parsley. Add the potatoes and combine gently so the potatoes are evenly covered with the dressing. Allow the salad to marinate for at least 2 hours at room temperature, or, covered and refrigerated, up to 24 hours.

Spread the potatoes on a platter. Garnish them with sliced egg, chunks of tuna, strips of pimiento and olives.

> **TIP:** Potatoes will slice without crumbling if you chill them before peeling and slicing.

Ensaladilla Rusa
"RUSSIAN" POTATO SALAD

Guy walks into a tapa bar in Bilbao. He looks over the "Neptune"—cuttlefish, ink sauce, bacon, rocket, cherry tomato with cuttlefish vinaigrette. He checks out the omelette of wild mushrooms and baby eels and the quail eggs with anchovy. Then he orders *ensaladilla rusa*, old-fashioned "Russian" salad, with potatoes, carrots and peas in mayonnaise. Guys will love this version.

Makes 18 tapas or 6 starters.

4 medium potatoes (785 g / 1 lb 2 oz)
3 carrots, peeled (160 g / 5 ½ oz)
75 g / 2 ½ oz / ½ cup fresh or frozen
    shelled peas
1 teaspoon salt
2 tablespoons extra virgin olive oil
2 piquillo peppers chopped (2 tablespoons)

1 hard-boiled egg, chopped
1 spring onion, finely chopped
3 tablespoons chopped pickle
1 teaspoon Dijon mustard
3 tablespoons chopped flat-leaf parsley
120 ml / 4 fl oz / ½ cup mayonnaise
3 tablespoons white wine vinegar

Cook the potatoes and carrots in boiling water to cover until tender. The carrots will take about 12 minutes; the potatoes a total of 20 minutes. Cook the peas until tender, about 10 minutes. Drain vegetables and chill them.

Peel the potatoes and cut them in 12 mm / ½ in dice. Cut the carrots lengthwise in quarters, then slice crosswise into small dice. Combine the potatoes, carrots and peas in a bowl. Add the salt, oil, chopped piquillo peppers, egg and onion.

In a small bowl combine the pickle, mustard, parsley, mayonnaise and vinegar. Whisk until smooth. Stir into the potatoes. Let the potatoes stand 2 hours at room temperature or, covered and refrigerated, up to 24 hours. Serve cold or room temperature.

Salpicón de Mariscos
SHELLFISH COCKTAIL

This makes a lovely starter for a dinner party. Turn it into a luxury version by substituting chunks of cooked lobster for the prawns and mussels. Sometimes it is made with chopped octopus or sliced fish roe. Some tapa bars use chunks of fake crab in the salpicón.

Makes 12 tapas or 6 starters.

450 g / 1 lb mussels, scrubbed and steamed open
250 g / 8 ¾ oz peeled prawns (shrimp)
3 ripe tomatoes, chopped
½ onion, chopped
1 green bell pepper, chopped
2 hard-boiled eggs, yolks separated from whites
1 clove garlic, crushed
6 tablespoons extra virgin olive oil
5 tablespoons wine vinegar
3 tablespoons chopped flat-leaf parsley
1 teaspoon salt
Lettuce leaves, to garnish
Sliced avocado, to garnish

Remove mussels from shells, discarding any that have not opened. Save a few on the half-shell for garnish. Cook the peeled prawns in boiling salted water for 1 minute and drain.

In a bowl combine the chopped tomatoes, onion, green pepper and chopped egg whites.

In a small bowl mash the egg yolks with the crushed garlic. Whisk in the oil, vinegar, parsley and salt.

Add the prawns and mussels to the tomato mixture. Stir in the dressing and chill, covered, until serving time. Serve on a platter garnished with lettuce, avocado and reserved mussels on the half-shell.

Alcachofas con Romesco y Butifarra
MARINATED ARTICHOKES WITH CATALAN SAUSAGE

The marinade for these artichokes is a quickie version of Catalan *romesco* sauce. It's a great dressing for just about any vegetable. *Butifarra* is a white, cooked Catalan sausage.

Makes 10 tapas.

2 teaspoons olive oil
40 g / 2 ½ oz skinned almonds
1 tablespoon pimentón (paprika)
½ teaspoon hot pimentón (spicy paprika) or
    dash of cayenne
Water
¼ cup flat-leaf parsley
3 cloves garlic
½ teaspoon salt
2 tablespoons vinegar

4 tablespoons extra virgin olive oil, preferably
    Arbequina
2 (400-g / 14-oz) packets frozen, cut-up
    artichokes
150 g / 5 oz *butifarra* sausage, casing removed
    and sliced
Salad leaves
1 hard-boiled egg, chopped
1 spring onion, chopped
Chopped fresh mint leaves

Heat 2 teaspoons oil in a small frying pan and fry the almonds until they are golden, 2 minutes. Reserve.

Place the two kinds of pimentón in a small bowl and stir in 4 tablespoons water. Place the parsley and garlic in a food processor and process until finely chopped. Add the almonds and process until smooth. Add the salt, vinegar, virgin olive oil, pimentón mixture and 4 tablespoons water. Process until the dressing is smooth.

Bring a pan of salted water to the boil and add the frozen artichokes. Cook until they are tender, about 6 minutes from the time the water returns to the boil. Drain well. Place the artichokes in a bowl and stir in the dressing. Allow to marinate at least 1 hour or, covered and refrigerated, up to 24 hours.

Fry the slices of sausage until lightly browned on both sides, 2 minutes. Add to the artichokes. Line a serving dish with salad leaves and spread the artichokes and sausage on top. Garnish with chopped egg, onion and mint. Serve cold or room temperature.

Garbanzos Aliñados
CHICKPEA SALAD WITH SAUSAGE

Start this recipe a day or two before serving, as you'll need to allow time to soak the chickpeas before cooking, then to marinate them in the oil and lemon dressing. *Salchichón* is a dry-cured sausage, somewhat like salami.

Short cut: Use two jars of ready-to-eat chickpeas instead of cooking them. Drain the liquid, rinse the chickpeas in water, then add the marinade.

Makes 6 tapas or 4 side dishes.

250 g / 9 oz chick peas, soaked overnight
1 bay leaf
1 slice onion
2 teaspoons salt
3 tablespoons extra virgin olive oil
3 tablespoons lemon juice
6 tablespoons chopped parsley
1 clove garlic, finely chopped

100 g / 3 ½ oz salchichón, cut in 10-mm / ⅜-in dice
1 spring onion, including some of the green part, chopped
3 tablespoons chopped red bell pepper
6 cherry tomatoes, halved
12 pitted black olives

Drain the chickpeas. Bring a pan of water to the boil and add the chickpeas. Skim off any foam that rises to the top. Add the bay leaf and onion slice. Cover and simmer 1 hour. Add the salt and simmer until chickpeas are tender, 1 hour more.

Drain the chickpeas, discarding the bay leaf and onion. Place them in a bowl and add the oil and lemon juice. Allow to marinate at least 2 hours and up to 24 hours.

Shortly before serving, add the parsley, garlic, salchichón, spring onion, bell pepper, tomatoes and olives. Add additional salt, if necessary. Serve cold or room temperature.

Ensalada de Pimientos Asados
ROASTED PEPPER SALAD

This is an all-time classic tapa, served all by itself or heaped on toast. It can also be a side dish or a condiment for sandwiches. It is usually made with sweet red bell peppers, but a few green ones add complexity of flavour.

Makes 8 to 10 tapas or side dishes.

6 bell peppers, red and/or green
1 clove finely chopped garlic
3 tablespoons extra virgin olive oil
3 tablespoons wine vinegar
Salt and pepper
Strips of tinned anchovies (optional)

Roast the peppers over a gas flame, over charcoal or under a grill (broiler), turning them until charred on all sides, 25 to 30 minutes. Remove them to a bowl and cover. Let stand 1 hour.

Peel off the skin from the peppers and cut away the stems and seeds. Tear the peppers into strips and put on a serving dish. Add the garlic, oil, vinegar, salt and pepper. Toss gently.

Serve the salad spread on a serving dish, topped with strips of anchovies, if desired.

Huevos Rellenos con Gambas
STUFFED EGGS WITH PRAWNS

You could use tinned tuna in place of the prawns to stuff the eggs.

Makes 16 tapas.

8 hard-boiled eggs
100 g / 3 ½ oz cooked, peeled and chopped prawns (shrimp)
3 tablespoons chopped pimiento-stuffed olives
2 teaspoons finely chopped onion
1 tablespoon chopped flat-leaf parsley
2 tablespoons lemon juice
¼ teaspoon salt
1 tablespoon olive oil
100 ml / 3 ½ fl oz / ⅓ cup mayonnaise
Strips of tinned red pimiento

Peel the eggs and cut them in half lengthwise. Remove the yolks and set aside. Remove a sliver from the bottom of the whites so they sit flat.

In a bowl, mash five of the yolks. Add the prawns, olives, onion, parsley, 1 tablespoon lemon juice, salt and oil and combine well. Spoon this mixture into the egg whites.

Stir the mayonnaise with the remaining lemon juice until it reaches spreading consistency. If necessary, thin with a little water. Top each egg with a frosting of mayonnaise. Grate the reserved yolks over the stuffed eggs. Lay a strip of red pimiento on top of each. Serve immediately or cover with plastic wrap and refrigerate until serving time.

Boquerones en Vinagre
MARINATED FRESH ANCHOVIES

Boquerones are tiny, fresh anchovies, famous on both the Mediterranean and Biscay coasts of Spain. For this famous tapa, the anchovies are filleted, then "cooked" in vinegar (no heat required), and dressed with garlic and olive oil. The filleting is easy, so have a go! Be sure to serve the anchovies accompanied by bread. Some tapa connoisseurs like to heap the little fish on the bread. Others prefer to eat the anchovies straight-up, with a cocktail stick or small fork, then dip the bread in the tangy dressing left on the plate.

Makes 12 tapas.

450 g / 1 lb whole, fresh anchovies
240 ml / 8 fl oz / 1 cup white wine vinegar
1 teaspoon salt
2 tablespoons extra virgin olive oil

3 cloves garlic, coarsely chopped
2 tablespoons chopped flat-leaf parsley
Shredded lettuce, to serve
Chopped spring onion, to garnish

Use a sharp knife to cut off the heads and pull out the innards of the fish. Then grasp the top of the spine with thumb and knife edge and pull the spine down across the belly of the fish. Cut off the spine, leaving the fillets attached at the tail. Wash and drain the anchovies.

Place the anchovies, skin-side down, in a single layer in a nonreactive container. Pour over the vinegar and ½ teaspoon of the salt. Cover and refrigerate for 24 hours or up to 48 hours.

Drain off all the vinegar marinade and rinse the anchovies in cold water. Drain them well. Arrange them skin-side down on a bed of shredded lettuce in a serving dish. Sprinkle with remaining salt, oil, garlic and parsley. Garnish with chopped onion.

For this famous tapa, the anchovies are filleted, then "cooked" in vinegar (no heat required), and dressed with garlic and olive oil.

Mejillones a la Vinagreta
MUSSELS VINAIGRETTE

Mussels can be steamed a day or two in advance of serving. Strain the liquid from the pan and pour it over the mussels to keep them moist. Cover tightly and refrigerate. Prepare the vinaigrette in advance too, then assemble the tapa right before serving.

Makes 24 tapas.

2 dozen mussels, scrubbed and beards removed
Shredded lettuce, for serving
2 tablespoons finely chopped spring onion
2 tablespoons finely chopped green bell pepper
2 tablespoons finely chopped red bell pepper
1 tablespoon chopped flat-leaf parsley
4 tablespoons extra virgin olive oil
2 tablespoons lemon juice
Dash of hot pepper sauce

Place mussels in a deep pan with a little water. Cover and place over high heat, shaking the pan, until mussels open, 3 to 4 minutes. Remove from heat and discard any mussels that do not open. When mussels are cool enough to handle, remove and discard the empty half-shells.

Place the mussels on a bed of shredded lettuce on a serving dish.

In a bowl, combine the onion, green and red peppers, parsley, oil, lemon juice and hot sauce. Spoon the vinaigrette over the mussels in their shells.

Caballa en Escabeche
FISH IN ESCABECHE MARINADE

A tangy marinade turns mackerel or other fish into a sophisticated starter. Serve chunks of the fish with salad greens and garnishes.

Makes 8 tapas or 6 starters.

4 fillets of mackerel, trout or lake perch
   (each about 300 g / 10 oz)
4 tablespoons olive oil
½ onion, sliced
½ red bell pepper, cut in thin strips
2 cloves garlic, slivered
1 carrot, peeled and sliced
200 ml / 6 fl oz / ¾ cup white wine vinegar
650 ml / 1 pint+2 fl oz / 2 ¾ cup water
¼ teaspoon peppercorns

¼ teaspoon oregano
4 tablespoons chopped flat-leaf parsley
2 teaspoons salt
1 bay leaf
1 small dry red chilli (optional)
Salad leaves for serving
Sprigs of parsley, for garnish
1 hard-boiled egg, quartered, for garnish
Sliced orange, for garnish
Extra virgin olive oil for serving

Cut each fillet into 4 pieces of similar size. Heat oil in a non-stick frying pan over medium heat and fry the fish until lightly browned, about 2 minutes per side. Remove the pieces and place them in one layer in a shallow nonreactive container.

Add the onion, pepper, garlic and carrot to the oil and sauté for 5 minutes. Add the vinegar, water, peppercorns, oregano, chopped parsley, salt, bay leaf and chilli. Bring to the boil and cook for 5 minutes.

Carefully pour the vinegar marinade with vegetables and spices over the fish. Allow to stand until cool. Cover and refrigerate for at least 12 and up to 36 hours.

To serve, lift the fish and vegetables out of the marinade with a slotted spoon and place them on top of salad leaves on a serving dish. Garnish with parsley sprigs, egg and orange slices. Drizzle over a little extra virgin oil. Serve cold or room temperature.

ChupaChups de Codorniz en Escabeche
LOLLIPOPS OF QUAIL IN ESCABECHE MARINADE

ChupaChups is a popular brand of lollipop. Eat these miniscule quail legs right off the bone like a lolly, a two-bite tapa. Leave drumstick and thigh connected. If you're cutting them from whole quail, use the breast fillets for seared quail with dates (page 149). This recipe can also be prepared using chicken drumettes, the thick, first joint of a chicken wing, instead of quail.

Makes 12 tapas.

12 whole quail legs (about 380 g / 13 ½ oz)
Salt and pepper
3 tablespoons olive oil
1 leek (white part only), sliced
1 carrot, sliced crosswise
1 slice of onion
1 slice of lemon
2 cloves garlic, slivered lengthwise
1 bay leaf

1 teaspoon pimentón (paprika) stirred into 1 tablespoon water
10 peppercorns
1 teaspoon oregano
2 teaspoons salt
240 ml / 8 fl oz / 1 cup water
120 ml / 4 fl oz / ½ cup white wine
120 ml / 4 fl oz / ½ cup wine vinegar
Salad leaves and cherry tomatoes, to serve

Sprinkle the quail legs with salt and pepper. Heat 1 tablespoon of oil in a frying pan on medium heat. Brown the quail on both sides, about 2 minutes. Remove. Wipe out the pan.

Add remaining 2 tablespoons of oil to the pan with the leek, carrot, onion, lemon, garlic, bay leaf, pimentón, peppercorns, oregano, salt, water, wine and vinegar. Bring to a boil.

Return the quail to the pan. Cover and simmer until quail is tender, but not falling off the bone, 12 to 15 minutes. Remove from heat and allow the quail to cool in the marinade.

Cover and refrigerate at least 24 hours or up to 48 hours. Serve cold or room temperature, garnished with salad leaves and tomatoes.

Gazpacho en Vasito
GAZPACHO IN A GLASS

Gazpacho, Andalusia's cold summer soup, turns up at tapa bars, served in tall glasses or mugs. Sipped from a glass, gazpacho should be about the consistency of cream. Omit the usual soup garnishes of chopped green peppers, onions and cucumbers. Serve this in small glasses or paper cups as a starter at your next patio barbecue party.

Serves 6 to 8.

4 slices bread, crusts removed (115 g / 4 oz)
2 cloves garlic
5 ripe tomatoes (about 900 g / 2 lb), peeled and seeded
Small piece of green bell pepper
¼ teaspoon ground cumin
2 teaspoons salt
6 tablespoons extra virgin olive oil
2 tablespoons white wine vinegar
350 ml / 12 fl oz / 1 ½ cups water
Thin strips of peeled cucumber and green pepper, for garnish

Break the bread into chunks and soak it in water to cover until softened. Squeeze out the water and place the bread in a blender or food processor with the garlic. Blend until smooth.

Add the tomatoes, green pepper, cumin and salt. With the blender running, add the oil in a slow stream. As the oil emulsifies, the gazpacho will turn from red to a pale orange colour. Blend in the vinegar and some of the water.

Place the gazpacho in a pitcher and add remaining water. Chill until serving time.

Stir the gazpacho and add additional water to thin it, if necessary. Serve the gazpacho into small glasses. Garnish with "swizzle sticks" of cucumber and green pepper.

Ajo Blanco con Uvas en Copitas
WHITE GAZPACHO SHOOTERS WITH GRAPES

Surprise your guests with this one—garlicky white gazpacho in shot glasses. It's a Málaga classic, garnished with sweet muscatel grapes, a brilliant contrast of flavours.

Makes 10 tapas.

6 slices day-old bread, crusts removed (170 g / 6 oz)
115 g / 4 oz / 1 cup blanched and skinned almonds
3 cloves garlic
120 ml / 4 fl oz / ½ cup extra virgin olive oil
5 tablespoons white wine vinegar
2 teaspoons salt
475 ml / 16 fl oz / 2 cups water
10 muscatel grapes

Soak the bread in water to cover until it is softened. Squeeze out the water and place in food processor or blender with the almonds and garlic. Pulse until the almonds are finely ground.

With the motor running, add the oil in a slow stream, then the vinegar and salt. Blend in some of the water, then pour the mixture into a pitcher and add remaining water.

Chill until serving time. Stir before serving. Pour into shot glasses. Spear grapes on cocktail sticks and place in each glass.

Gambas Cocidas / Langostinos Cocidos
COOKED PRAWNS

Tapa bars stake their reputations on serving the freshest prawns (shrimp), simply boiled. You peel the prawns yourself, suck the heads (because that's where the delicious roe is), peel the tails and eat them with absolutely no additional sauce.

Gambas and *langostinos* are two types of prawns (shrimp). Use whole prawns, preferably with heads and tails intact.

For every 225 g / 8 oz of prawns that you are cooking, use 1 litre / 1 ¾ pints / 4 ¼ cups water and 30 g / 1 oz / 2 tablespoons salt. Bring water to the boil in a large pan. Have ready a pan of ice water. Add the prawns to the boiling water. Cook small prawns for 1 minute; king prawns (jumbo shrimp) for 2 to 3 minutes. Skim the prawns out of the boiling water and into the ice water. When cool, drain the prawns. They're ready to serve.

La Tortilla y Más

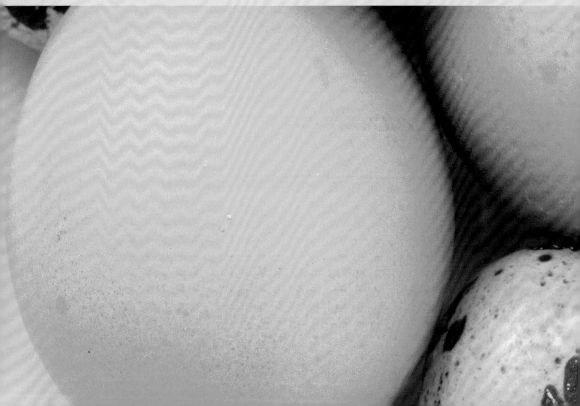

POTATO TORTILLA & MORE EGG DISHES

La Tortilla y Más
POTATO TORTILLA AND MORE EGG DISHES

Spanish Tortilla (*Tortilla de Patatas*)

Potato Tortilla with Chorizo and Chard
(*Tortilla de Patatas con Chorizo y Acelgas*)

Aubergine Tortilla (*Tortilla de Berenjena*)

"Dismantled" Eggs with Baby Broad Beans and Ham
(*Huevos Desmontados con Habitas y Jamón*)

Eggs Scrambled With Mushrooms, Prawns and Green Garlic
(*Huevos Revueltos Con Setas, Gambas y Ajetes*)

"Broken" Eggs with Potatoes and Garlic
(*Huevos Rotos con Patatas y Ajo*)

Eggs Scrambled with Asparagus
(*Revuelto de Esparragos*)

The tortilla is Spain's great egg dish, the most emblematic tapa of all. A tortilla is round, flat and fairly thick, like a cake, with the filling (usually potatoes) incorporated in the eggs. Unlike the Italian *frittata*, which it somewhat resembles, the tortilla isn't finished in the oven. It cooks entirely in a frying pan. The cooking medium is always olive oil, never butter.

Beyond the classic potato tortilla are embellishments and regional variations. Some of these are *tortilla Sacromonte*, famous in Granada, made with brains, lamb's or calves' testicles, ham and peas; *tortilla de escabeche*, a Madrid favourite, with pickled tuna incorporated in the eggs, and *tortilla capuchina*, with asparagus, bread crumbs and potatoes. Then, too, avant-garde chefs have had some fun with the traditional tortilla, deconstructing its component ingredients into new forms—potato foam, onion dust, olive oil ice cream, egg yolk custard—and putting them back together in a cocktail glass or soup bowl. You get the idea.

Beyond tortilla is another group of egg dishes that also are popular tapas. These are *revueltos*, eggs scrambled with vegetables, potatoes, sausage, meat or prawns. To serve them as a tapa, heap the eggs on toast. Or, make them the main dish for brunch or lunch.

Tortilla de Patatas
POTATO TORTILLA

Some tapa bars present super-size tortillas, almost 60 cm / 2 ft in diameter and more than 7 cm / 3 in thick. They are cut into thick squares and served with bread. Tortilla also makes a nice supper dish and is grand packed in a picnic hamper. In Spain, tortilla is rarely served with a sauce, but might be paired with a juicy vegetable dish such as *pisto* (page 163). If you do want a sauce, look in Sauces, Dressings, Dips and Spreads.

Makes 12 tapas or 4 main dishes.

120 ml / 4 fl oz / ½ cup olive oil
1 kg / 2 ¼ lb potatoes (about 4 large), peeled and thinly sliced
2 tablespoons chopped onion (optional)
6 eggs
1 teaspoon salt

Heat the oil in a no-stick or well-seasoned frying pan (26 cm / 10 in). Add the sliced potatoes and turn them in the oil. Let them cook slowly in the oil, without browning, turning frequently. If using onions, add them when the potatoes are partially cooked. The potatoes will take 20 to 30 minutes to cook.

Meanwhile, beat the eggs in a bowl with the salt.

Place a plate over the potatoes and drain off excess oil into a small heatproof bowl. Add the potatoes to the beaten eggs and combine well. Add a little of the reserved oil to the frying pan and pour in the potato-egg mixture. Cook on a medium heat without stirring until set, about 5 minutes. Regulate the heat so the tortilla does not get too brown on the bottom Shake the pan to keep the tortilla from sticking.

Place a flat lid or plate over the pan, hold it tightly, and reverse the tortilla onto the plate. Add a little more oil to the pan, if necessary, and slide the tortilla back in to cook on the reverse side, about 3 minutes more. Slide out onto a serving plate.

Cut into squares for tapas or slice in wedges as a main dish. Serve hot or room temperature.

Tortilla de Patatas con Chorizo y Acelgas
POTATO TORTILLA WITH CHORIZO AND CHARD

The addition of chopped chorizo and chard leaves makes this a much more substantial dish than the classic tortilla. Serve it for breakfast or lunch.

Makes 20 tapas or 4 main dishes.

120 ml / 4 fl oz / ½ cup olive oil
1 kg / 2 ¼ lb potatoes (about 4 large), peeled and diced
150 g / 5 ¼ oz chard leaves, chopped

2 tablespoons chopped onion
85 g / 3 oz chorizo, cut in 10 mm / ⅜ in dice
1 teaspoon salt
6 eggs

Heat the oil in a 28-cm / 11-in no-stick frying pan over medium heat. Add the potatoes, turn them in the oil, then reduce heat and let them cook slowly, without browning, 15 minutes.

Meanwhile, blanch the chopped chard in boiling water for 5 minutes. Drain well.

Add the onion, diced chorizo, chard and half of the salt to the potatoes in the pan. Continue cooking potatoes until they are completely tender, 15 minutes longer.

Beat the eggs in a large bowl with the remaining salt.

Place a large plate on top of the pan of potatoes. Holding the plate tightly, carefully tip the pan and drain the oil into a small heatproof bowl. Stir the potatoes, chard and chorizo into the beaten eggs.

Return a spoonful of oil to the pan over medium heat. Pour in the egg-potato mixture. Spread it evenly. Reduce heat and cook, without stirring, until the tortilla is set on the bottom, about 5 minutes. Do not allow the bottom to brown too much. You can shake the pan occasionally to make sure the tortilla doesn't stick on the bottom.

Again, place the plate on top of the pan. Working over a bowl to catch any drips, hold the plate tightly in place and turn the pan upside down, reversing the tortilla onto the plate. Slide the tortilla back into the frying pan. Let it cook on the bottom, 2 minutes.

Lift the front edge of the tortilla and carefully slide it out of the pan onto a serving dish or cutting board. Cut into 5-cm / 2-in squares to serve as a tapa or into wedges if serving as a lunch dish. Serve hot or room temperature.

Tortilla de Berenjena
AUBERGINE TORTILLA

This tortilla is not as thick as the classic one with potatoes, because the aubergines and peppers cook down quite a bit. This makes a great sandwich filling.

Makes 8 tapas or 4 main dishes.

1 red bell pepper
1 green bell pepper
4 tablespoons olive oil
¼ onion, chopped
3 tomatoes, peeled, seeded and chopped
1 small aubergine (eggplant), peeled and diced
6 eggs
½ teaspoon salt

Roast the peppers under the grill (broiler), turning them, until they are charred on all sides, 25 to 30 minutes. Remove them to a plate and cover with a lid. Let stand until cool enough to handle. Remove skin, stems and seeds and tear peppers into strips.

Heat 2 tablespoons of the oil in a frying pan over medium heat and sauté the onion. Add the tomatoes, peppers and aubergine and continue cooking until aubergine is tender and most of the liquid has cooked away, about 15 minutes.

Beat the eggs and salt in a bowl. Mix the fried aubergine mixture into the eggs.

Wipe out the frying pan. Heat the remaining oil and pour in the egg mixture. Cook, without browning, until the tortilla is set on the bottom, about 4 minutes. Reverse it onto a plate and slide it back into the pan to cook the reverse side, about 2 minutes. Cut into wedges and serve hot or room temperature.

Huevos Desmontados con Habitas y Jamón
"DISMANTLED" EGGS WITH BABY BROAD BEANS AND HAM

This is a favourite tapa In the Cava Baja district of Madrid, where tascas are chock-a-block. If you've got the beans already sautéed with the ham, it only takes a couple of minutes to break in the eggs and stir them around. Be sure to serve this tapa accompanied by bread or toast.

Makes 6 tapas.

300 g / 11 oz shelled baby broad beans (fava beans)
3 tablespoons olive oil
¼ onion, chopped
1 clove garlic, chopped
60 g / 2 oz serrano ham, chopped
Salt and pepper
6 eggs

Bring a pan of water to the boil and add the beans. Blanch them for 2 minutes and drain.

Heat the oil in a cazuela (earthenware casserole) or frying pan and sauté the onion and garlic 3 minutes. Add the ham and beans and sauté 5 minutes, or until beans are tender. Season with salt and pepper.

Push the beans aside and break the eggs into the pan. Allow the whites to cook. Remove the pan from the heat and stir to break up the yolks. Serve hot.

Huevos Revueltos Con Setas, Gambas y Ajetes
EGGS SCRAMBLED WITH MUSHROOMS, PRAWNS AND GREEN GARLIC

Serve this egg dish as a starter or as a light supper dish. Green garlic shoots look like miniature spring onions and have a mild flavour. If they are not available, substitute leeks, very finely chopped and blanched in boiling water. In Spain this dish is made with any one of several types of wild mushrooms, but you could use cultivated white mushrooms instead.

Makes 6 tapas or 4 starters.

150 g / 5 oz mushrooms (such as chanterelles, oyster mushrooms or boletus)
6 to 8 green garlic shoots or ½ leek
3 tablespoons olive oil
150 g / 5 oz peeled, raw prawns (shrimp)
1 tbsp water
6 eggs
Salt and pepper
Squares of fried bread, to serve

Cut away any woody parts of the mushrooms, rinse under running water and pat them dry on a kitchen towel. Slice the mushrooms. Trim off ends of garlic shoots and chop them, including the green shoots. Heat the oil in a frying pan and sauté the mushrooms and garlic until softened. Add the prawns and sauté 1 minute.

Beat together the water, eggs, salt and pepper. Pour into the mushrooms and cook, stirring, until eggs are set creamy-soft. Serve immediately with fried bread.

Huevos Rotos con Patatas y Ajo
"BROKEN" EGGS WITH POTATOES AND GARLIC

This peasant dish, studded with whole cloves of garlic, turns up at Madrid's trendiest tapa bars—the perfect foil for robust red wine.

Makes 8 tapas or 4 main dishes.

900 g / 2 lb baking potatoes (about 4)
6 cloves garlic
6 tablespoons olive oil
6 tablespoons chopped spring onions
½ green bell pepper, chopped

Pinch of red chilli flakes or cayenne
1 teaspoon salt
¼ teaspoon ground cumin
4 eggs
2 tablespoons chopped parsley

Peel the potatoes. Cut them lengthwise into quarters, then slice them crosswise. Crush the garlic lightly with the flat side of a knife, just to split the skins. Slice off the tops, but do not peel them.

Heat the oil in a large non-stick frying pan. Add the potatoes and garlic and sauté on medium-high heat for 5 minutes. Don't let the potatoes brown.

Add the onions, green pepper, red chilli flakes, salt and cumin. Sauté on a high heat for 1 minute. Cover and lower heat. Cook, stirring occasionally, until potatoes are tender, about 15 minutes.

Push the potatoes to one side and break an egg into the pan. Move potatoes again and add another egg. Likewise, add two more eggs. Let the eggs cook on a medium heat for 2 minutes until the whites are set. Sprinkle with parsley.

With a wooden spoon, scoop up and turn the potatoes, breaking up the eggs. Make four or five turns. Remove the pan from the heat. Cover and allow the eggs to finish cooking in the heat from the potatoes, 2 minutes. Serve hot.

Revuelto de Esparragos
EGGS SCRAMBLED WITH ASPARAGUS

Sometimes this is prepared with thin stalks of wild asparagus, which has a slightly bitter flavour. Serve the eggs with bread fried in olive oil as an accompaniment.

Makes 6 tapas, 4 starters or 2 main dishes.

450 g / 1 lb trimmed and chopped green asparagus
2 tablespoons olive oil
½ onion, chopped
1 clove chopped garlic
30 g /1 oz chopped serrano ham or bacon
4 eggs
½ teaspoon salt
Freshly ground black pepper
Fried bread, to serve

Cook the chopped asparagus in boiling, salted water until cooked to desired doneness, 5 to15 minutes. Drain.

In a frying pan heat the oil and sauté the onion, garlic and ham until onion is slightly softened. Stir in the drained asparagus and sauté gently for 5 minutes.

Beat the eggs in a bowl with 1 tablespoon of water and the salt. Stir the eggs into the skillet. Keep stirring them on a medium heat until soft-set. Remove and serve immediately with freshly ground black pepper and pieces of fried bread as an accompaniment.

A La Plancha

FOODS ON THE GRIDDLE

A La Plancha
FOODS ON THE GRIDDLE

Prawns on the Griddle (*Langostinos a la Plancha*)

Griddled Baby Cuttlefish (*Chopitos a la Plancha*)

Mini Kebabs with Moorish Spices (*Pinchitos Morunos*)

Seared Beef Cutlets with Mushrooms (*Pepito con Setas*)

Griddled Pork Cutlets (*Planchitas de Cerdo*)

Griddled Baby Lamb Chops (*Chuletitas de Cordero a la Plancha*)

Seared Tuna with Onion Confit (*Atún con Cebollas Confitadas*)

Swordfish Kebabs (*Brochetas de Pez Espada*)

Seared Duck Breast with Two Sauces (*Magret de Pato a la Parilla*)

Seared Quail Breasts with Dates (*Pechugitas de Codorniz con Dátiles*)

Griddled Vegetables (*Verduras a la Plancha*)

Some tapa bars are brash, florescent-lit, noisy and crowded. What's the appeal? Perch on a bar stool and watch while a griddle meister manages six or eight different orders on a couple of *planchas*, big flat griddles. (A plancha is the same sort of griddle you might find in a fast-food joint for cooking hamburgers.) He's griddling tiny squid; whole, unpeeled prawns; slabs of swordfish steak; pork cutlets, and small steaks, basting them with *aliño*, a mixture of olive oil, garlic, parsley and lemon. Some of the locals standing at the bar appear to be eating a whole lunch—seared swordfish steaks with sides of *patatas bravas*, crispy potato cubes, and salad.

So you see why these bars are so popular? Top-quality foods, very simply prepared. No fancy sauces. Beer or wine to accompany. No wonder the place is packed. It doesn't need ambience.

A plancha is a great tool for home cooking. Choose either a heavy, cast-iron griddle (grill pan in America), which heats evenly, or one of the newer types with no-stick surfaces. Especially useful is a reversible one—ridged griddle (grill pan) on one side, great for steaks, and flat griddle on the other, perfect for fish and shellfish. Round, oval or rectangular, the plancha sets directly over a gas hob (burner). Big ones are placed over two gas rings. The best substitute for a griddle is a heavy, cast-iron frying pan.

Most foods that are cooked on a plancha can also be cooked *a la parilla*, on a barbecue (grill).

Confused by the terminology? Here's a translation:

Spanish	British	American
parilla, gratinador	grill	broiler
plancha	griddle, hot plate	grill pan, griddle
asar a la parilla, brasa	barbecue	grill

Langostinos a la Plancha
PRAWNS ON THE GRIDDLE

Griddle cooking is all about flavour, so use fresh, not frozen, prawns. Allow six whole king prawns (jumbo shrimp) (100 g / 3 ½ oz) per serving. You can probably fit a dozen prawns on a standard-sized griddle. A true master of the griddle puts the basting oil in a squeeze bottle. That way the oil never comes into contact with the prawns and so can be used over and over. However, if you are making prawns on a single occasion, put the oil mixture in a small bowl and use a brush to dab it on the prawns. Throw out any remaining oil mixture.

Each person peels the prawns for himself—messy, but ever so satisfying. Provide guests with finger bowls or serviettes to clean fingers. Sauce is optional—consider *romesco*, Catalan red pepper sauce, (page 242) or *alioli*, garlic mayonnaise, (pages 248 and 250) as an accompaniment to the prawns.

Serves 6.

120 ml / 4 fl oz / ½ cup olive oil
3 tablespoons wine vinegar
2 teaspoons salt
600 g / 1 lb 5 oz whole, unpeeled king prawns (jumbo shrimp)

Combine the oil, vinegar and salt.

Heat a griddle or heavy frying pan until very hot. Place the prawns on the griddle, drizzle or brush them with the oil-vinegar mixture and cook 2 minutes. Turn the prawns, drizzle again with oil and cook 1 minute longer. Serve immediately.

Chopitos a la Plancha
GRIDDLED BABY CUTTLEFISH

This is the sort of tapa to order by the *ración*, plateful, and share around the table. These tiny cuttlefish, griddled whole—ink and all—are messy, but ever so delicious.

Makes 4 tapas.

260 g / 9 oz small (5 cm / 2 in) cuttlefish (about 30)
Olive oil for griddle
Salt
3 tablespoons *aliño* (sauce for griddled foods, page 255)

Wash the cuttlefish and pat them dry. Leave them whole. Brush a griddle with oil and sprinkle lightly with salt. Heat until very hot. Lay the cuttlefish on the griddle in one layer and cook until browned on both sides, about 3 minutes.

Place the cuttlefish on a serving dish and spoon the aliño over them. Serve immediately.

Pinchitos Morunos
MINI KEBABS WITH MOORISH SPICES

These mini kebabs are popular in Málaga and Cádiz tapa bars. Exotic Moorish spices from nearby Morocco give the meat—usually pork—a lot of flavour. In Spain, spice vendors sell a ready-mixed blend, *especia para pinchitos*, pinchito spice, which contains lots of cumin, coriander, red chilli, turmeric and ginger. If you can´t get the spice mix, use instead a spoonful of Madras curry powder combined with an equal quantity of ground cumin seed.

The meat must be cut in quite small pieces, so that it cooks in the few minutes it takes to brown. Thin metal skewers work best (buy them in a *ferretería*, hardware store), and can be reused. If using bamboo skewers, soak them first in water and take care that they don´t come in contact with the heated griddle.

Makes 16 mini kebabs.

1 tablespoon ground cumin
1 tablespoon Madras curry powder
900 g / 2 lb boneless pork shoulder, cut in 18-mm / ¾-in cubes
6 tablespoons chopped parsley
10 cloves garlic, chopped
2 teaspoons salt
120 ml / 4 fl oz / ½ cup fresh lemon juice

Combine the cumin and curry powder. Place half the cubes of pork in a non-reactive bowl and sprinkle with half the parsley, garlic, salt, spice mixture and lemon juice. Add remaining pork, then remaining parsley, garlic, salt, spice and lemon juice. Marinate, covered and refrigerated, for 24 hours. Turn the meat 2 or 3 times.

Thread 4 or 5 pieces of meat onto thin metal skewers. Cook them on a hot griddle, turning until browned on all sides, 7 to 8 minutes.

Pepito con Setas
SEARED BEEF CUTLETS WITH MUSHROOMS

This is fast food! The beef cutlets cook in less than two minutes. Use very thinly sliced rump steak or topside to prepare these cutlets. Trim away the fat.

Makes 10 tapas.

300 g / 10 ½ oz thinly sliced beef
Salt and pepper
Pinch of oregano
2 cloves garlic, chopped
Olive oil
170 g / 6 oz oyster mushrooms
Thinly sliced tomatoes
10 slices bread, to serve

Use a wooden meat mallet to pound the beef to even thickness, about 5 mm / ⅛ in. Cut the slices into10 small cutlets, each about 75 mm X 50 mm / 3 in X 2 in. Spread the cutlets on a plate and sprinkle with salt, pepper, oregano and chopped garlic. Drizzle them with 2 tablespoons oil. Allow to stand at room temperature for 30 minutes.

Clean mushrooms and trim away woody stems. Leave small ones whole. Cut large ones in half, making about 10 pieces.

Brush a griddle with oil and heat very hot. Place the cutlets on the griddle until browned on one side, about 40 seconds. Turn and cook the other side, 40 seconds. Remove.

Brush griddle with additional oil. Place the mushrooms on it and griddle them about 2 minutes per side.

Stack a slice of tomato, a cutlet and a mushroom on each bread slice. Serve immediately.

VARIATION:

To prepare *planchitas de cerdo*, griddled pork cutlets, use thinly sliced pork steaks and trim them as for the beef, above. Marinate 30 minutes with salt, pepper, chopped garlic, chopped parsley, lemon juice and olive oil. Cook on a hot griddle, about 60 seconds per side. Serve with bread.

Chuletitas de Cordero a la Plancha
GRIDDLED BABY LAMB CHOPS

In Spain, baby lamb is a delicacy. Whole ones are roasted in wood-burning ovens. Tapa bars serve tiny baby lamb chops, quickly cooked on the plancha. Each chop provides a single bite of exquisite flavour. At their best, the chops are trimmed so that the cleaned bones serve as "handles," perfect for serving as finger food. However, when you buy chops, every other chop will have no bone at all. So adapt this recipe to suit your guests. Serve with knife and fork if "handle" is not available.

Makes 8 tapas or 4 main dishes.

680 g / 1 ½ lb baby lamb chops (about 16)
Salt and pepper
Pinch of thyme
2 tablespoons lemon juice
Olive oil for the griddle
Garlic mayonnaise with quince (page 250)

Trim away fat from the bones of the chops, leaving bones clean and nugget of flesh. Season them with salt, pepper, thyme and lemon juice. Allow to stand 30 minutes.

Brush griddle with oil and heat very hot. Cook the chops until browned on both sides, 3 minutes for medium-rare, 4 minutes for well-done.

Serve the chops immediately accompanied by garlic mayonnaise with quince.

Atún con Cebollas Confitadas
SEARED TUNA WITH ONION CONFIT

Both in Andalusia and in the Basque Country, *atún encebollado* is a favourite tapa. It consists of tuna braised with lots and lots of onions. This is a modernised version. The tuna is flash-cooked on the griddle and served with a deeply flavourful onion sauce. You should get to know Don Pedro Ximénez, aka PX. The sweet wines made from this grape varietal add alluring caramel and figgy flavours to sauces. If you can´t find PX wine, use a medium Málaga Muscatel or oloroso Sherry.

Makes 10 tapas or 2 main dishes.

2 onions
3 tablespoons olive oil plus additional for the griddle
1 clove garlic, chopped
Pinch of grated orange zest
150 ml / ¼ pint / 5 fl oz PX wine
1 tablespoon Sherry vinegar
300 g / 10 ½ oz tuna steak, 3 cm / 1 ¼ in thick
Salt and pepper
1 tablespoon orange juice

Cut the onions in half, then slice them thinly crosswise. Heat the oil in a frying pan and add the onions and garlic. Cook very slowly, stirring frequently, until onions are dark brown, 40 minutes. Do not let them scorch.

Add the orange zest, PX wine and vinegar. Simmer another 10 minutes, until the sauce is syrupy. Reserve.

While onions are cooking, season the tuna with salt and pepper and sprinkle with orange juice. Allow to stand at room temperature 30 minutes.

Heat a ridged griddle (grill pan) and brush with oil. Cook the tuna steak 1 to 2 minutes per side, or until browned on the surface but still pink on the inside. Remove and let rest 5 minutes.

Use a sharp knife to remove and discard skin and dark section of tuna meat. Cut into 10 squares, approximately 4 cm / 1 ½ in. Stick each piece on a cocktail stick and spoon over the onion confit. Serve warm or room temperature.

Brochetas de Pez Espada
SWORDFISH KEBABS

Made with perfectly fresh swordfish, this hardly needs a sauce embellishment. (Don't even consider frozen fish—it will taste like cardboard.) If you can get thin metal skewers, use them. Bamboo ones need to be soaked in water, but, even so, they may burn if they touch the griddle. You can prepare these kebabs with other firm-fleshed fish such as tuna, angler or grouper. Double these quantities to make four main dish servings.

Makes 10 tapas or 2 main dishes.

300 g / 10 ½ oz swordfish steak, cut 12 mm / ½ in thick
2 cloves garlic, chopped
2 tablespoons fresh lemon juice
1 tablespoon olive oil plus additional for griddle
2 tablespoons chopped flat-leaf parsley
½ teaspoon salt
1 green bell pepper, cut in small squares
Lemon wedges, to serve

Trim off skin from the swordfish steaks. Cut them in half lengthwise, then crosswise into 3-cm / 1 ¼-in squares, making approximately 20 pieces. Place them in a shallow bowl and add the garlic, lemon juice, oil, parsley and salt. Marinate at room temperature for 30 minutes.

Soak 10 bamboo skewers in water.

Thread a square of swordfish, a square of green pepper and another square of swordfish on each skewer.

Heat a griddle until hot and brush with oil. Cook the kebabs, turning them once, until lightly browned, about 1 minute per side. Serve immediately, accompanied by lemon wedges.

Magret de Pato a la Parilla
SEARED DUCK BREAST WITH TWO SAUCES

A flat plancha (griddle) doesn´t work for this duck breast, as a great deal of fat is rendered from the meat. Use a heavy frying pan instead. Duck breast is usually served very rare. Both the tangy olive sauce and the sweet fig sauce complement the rich duck meat. Take your pick.

Makes 12 tapas or 3 main dishes.

1 boneless duck breast (*magret*), 420 to 450 g / 15 to 16 oz
Coarse salt
Freshly ground black pepper
2 teaspoons Sherry vinegar
Olive sauce (page 245) or fig sauce (page 244)

Use a sharp knife to score the fatty side of the duck breast in a diagonal cross-hatch, without cutting into the flesh. Sprinkle generously with salt and pepper and Sherry vinegar. Allow to stand at room temperature for 30 minutes.

Heat a heavy frying pan on medium-high heat. Sear the duck breast, fat side down, until fat is crisped and browned, 6 to 8 minutes.

Very carefully drain off excess fat. Turn the duck breast and cook until browned, 3 to 4 minutes. Turn the breast on end to brown the edges. The duck should be browned on the outside and rare in the centre.

Remove and allow to stand 10 minutes. Place on a cutting board and carve crosswise into 10-mm / ⅜-in slices. Serve the slices topped with olive sauce or fig sauce. Serve hot.

Pechugitas de Codorniz con Dátiles
SEARED QUAIL BREASTS WITH DATES

Wrapping the delicate quail breasts in bacon both flavours them and keeps them juicy. A sliver of date under the wraps adds a surprise burst of sweetness. Take care not to overcook the quail—it should still be pink in the centre.

Makes 12 tapas.

12 boneless quail breast halves (275 g / 10 oz)
Salt and freshly ground black pepper
Pinch of pimentón (paprika)
Pinch of thyme
2 cloves garlic, chopped
6 pitted dates, halved lengthwise
6 thick slices bacon (180 g / 6 oz)
Olive oil for the griddle

Place the quail breasts on a plate in a single layer. Sprinkle them with salt, pepper, pimentón, thyme and chopped garlic. Allow to stand 30 minutes.

Flatten the dates and place half a date on top of each quail breast. Remove bacon rinds and cut the slices in half crosswise. Wrap each breast in a bacon strip and fasten with a wooden toothpick.

Brush a griddle with oil and heat. Cook the wrapped quail breasts until bacon is browned on both sides and quail is still pink in the centre, about 6 minutes. Serve hot.

Verduras a la Plancha
GRIDDLED VEGETABLES

This assortment of vegetables cooked on the plancha makes a good starter, in place of a salad. Use either a ridged or a flat griddle. Cooking time will vary for each vegetable, depending on thickness, but all should cook in 8 minutes or less. Cook the aubergine very tender, but allow asparagus and onion to stay somewhat crisp. The vegetables are delicious with nothing more elaborate than extra virgin olive oil. However, if you like, serve *alioli*, garlic mayonnaise (page 248), as an accompaniment.

Makes 8 tapas or 4 starters.

1 medium aubergine (eggplant) (225 g / 8 oz)
1 medium courgette (zucchini) (340 g / 12 oz)
Coarse salt
4 tablespoons olive oil
2 red bell peppers
8 asparagus spears

1 onion (or spears of spring onions)
4 mushrooms, such as portabello, oyster, or boletus
2 firm plum tomatoes, quartered
4 teaspoons extra virgin olive oil

Peel the aubergine and cut off the stem end. Cut lengthwise into 18- mm / ¾-in thick slices. Place in a shallow pan. Trim ends of courgette and slice it lengthwise into 12-mm / ½-in thick slices. Place in a single layer in the pan. Sprinkle aubergine and courgette on both sides with salt. Let stand 1 hour. Drain the aubergine and courgette in a colander 15 minutes. Pat dry.

Wipe out the shallow pan. Spread the aubergine and courgette slices in it. Brush them on both sides with oil.

Cut the peppers into quarters, discarding stem and seeds. Use a vegetable peeler to shave outer skins from asparagus. Slice onion 12 mm / ½ in thick. Spread pepper, asparagus, onion, mushrooms, tomato, and garlic in another shallow pan and brush them with oil.

Brush a ridged or flat griddle (grill pan) with oil and heat very hot. Cook each of the vegetables until tender, turning them with tongs to cook both sides. Aubergine will need about 8 minutes; courgette, 6; asparagus, 8; onion, 5; mushrooms, 8; tomato, 3.

Arrange vegetables on plates. Sprinkle with coarse salt and drizzle with extra virgin olive oil. Serve warm or room temperature.

Cazuelitas

SAUCY DISHES

Cazuelitas
SAUCY DISHES

Cazuela Cookery

Artichokes with Ham and Córdoba Wine
(*Alcachofas a la Cordobesa*)

Artichoke How-To

Spinach with Chickpeas (*Espinacas con Garbanzos*)

Broad Beans Sautéed with Ham (*Habas Salteadas con Jamón*)

Mushrooms Sautéed with Garlic (*Champiñones al Ajillo*)

Vegetable Medley (*Pisto*)

Potato Casserole (*Patatas a lo Pobre*)

Potatoes, La Rioja Style (*Patatas a la Riojana*)

Potatoes with Importance (*Patatas a la Importancia*)

Mussels, Fishermen's Style (*Mejillones a la Marinera*)

Mussel Bound

Prawns Sizzled with Garlic (*Gambas al Ajillo*)

Piquillo Peppers Stuffed with Prawns
(*Pimientos de Piquillo Rellenos con Gambas*)

Crab Gratin (*Txangurro*)

Scallop Gratin (*Vieiras Gratinadas*)

Clams with Beans (*Almejas con Fabes*)

Fish Balls in Sauce (*Albondiguitas de Pescado*)

Shellfish Balls in Green Sauce (*Albóndigas de Mariscos en Salsa Verde*)

Cuttlefish with Broad Beans (*Chocos con Habas*)

Sausage Bites in Sherry (*Bocados de Chorizo al Jerez*)

Pimentón—Ruddy Good

Kidneys in Sherry Sauce (*Riñones al Jerez*)

Pork with Tomato (*Magro con Tomate*)

Chicken Sautéed with Garlic (*Pollo al Ajillo*)

Meatballs in Almond Sauce (*Albóndigas en Salsa de Almendras*)

Oxtail Stew (*Estofado de Rabo de Toro*)

Black Rice with Shellfish (*Arroz Negro con Mariscos*)

Squid How-To

Rice and Seafood, Sevilla Style (*Cazuela de Arroz con Mariscos a la Sevillana*)

Rice How-To

cazuelitas
SAUCY DISHES

Cazuelitas are little earthenware dishes, perfect for individual servings of foods with sauce or stews. Some tapas, such as prawns sizzled with garlic, are cooked right in the cazuelita and served straight to the table. Other dishes and stews are cooked in a large cazuela, then dished into smaller portions to serve.

Ranging from vegetables to seafood to meat and poultry, these are also called *tapas de cocina,* "tapas from the kitchen," or cooked dishes, usually served hot. Many are foods cooked with sauce, which require a spoon (but not a knife and fork) to eat them. Plus, of course, chunks of bread for mopping up the sauces.

Many main-course dishes are transformed into tapas by serving them in individual cazuelitas. Oxtail stew, meatballs, potage of chickpeas and spinach, even paella are a few examples. Soups sometimes turn up as tapas as well. In Madrid taverns, the grand *cocido,* a one-pot stew with meat, sausage, vegetables, chickpeas and broth, is served in miniature terra-cotta pots.

If you like serving tapas, now's the time to get a batch of inexpensive cazuelitas. They're perfect for serving olives and nuts as well as individual tapas. If you haven't got a collection of cazuelitas, use any small dish, ramekin, or shallow bowl. Pretty glazed ceramic ashtrays can be converted to tapas serving dishes. Mix and match.

CAZUELA COOKERY

A traditional earthenware cazuela, or casserole, is made of low-fired clay—terra cotta. It is glazed on the inside, so liquids don't escape through the porous clay, and unglazed on the outside. Cazuelas come in many widths, though they generally are not very deep. For example, a 25-cm / 10-in cazuela is only 7 ½ cm / 3 in deep. They can be used on a gas or electric hob (top of stove) and in the oven. Big ones are heavy and not easy to manoeuvre in and out of the oven. Small ones, cazuelitas, are perfect for individual servings.

You can use a cazuela in place of a frying pan, a paella pan, a stewing pan, a sauté pan. The advantage of cazuela cooking is that earthenware holds a slow, steady heat, allowing food to cook gently and evenly. Because earthenware holds the heat, food continues to cook even after you remove it from the heat. You can even sauté and brown foods in a cazuela. Just add enough oil to cover the bottom surface and heat the oil until it's very hot. This will take longer than in a metal frying pan. Be sure not to crowd the pan with the foods to be browned.

New cazuelas taste of raw clay. Soak them in water for 24 hours, then dry well and rub with olive oil. Place in a medium-low oven for 40 minutes. Frequent use is the best method for curing earthenware.

> The advantage of cazuela cooking is that earthenware holds a slow, steady heat, allowing food to cook gently and evenly.

Don't heat a cazuela empty and take care not to set a hot one down on a cold surface, as it might crack. Cazuelas and cazuelitas are safe to use in the microwave, so prepared dishes can be quickly reheated.

Alcachofas a la Cordobesa
ARTICHOKES WITH HAM AND CÓRDOBA WINE

This is a favourite dish in the tabernas of Córdoba. The artichokes are first sautéed, then simmered in Córdoba wine, the dry fino of Montilla-Moriles, which is similar to Sherry fino. Supposedly artichokes don't pair well with wine, but fino, whether from Montilla-Moriles or Jerez, makes a perfect match. Artichokes prepared in this manner make a good starter. Tossed with spaghetti or noodles, they become a main dish.

This recipe is streamlined with the use of frozen artichokes. If you'd like to try it with fresh ones, see the how-to section.

Makes 8 tapas or starters.

2 (400 g / 14 oz) packets frozen, cut-up artichokes
Pinch of saffron threads
4 tablespoons hot water
4 tablespoons olive oil
4 cloves garlic, sliced crosswise
2 tablespoons chopped onion

60 g / 2 oz chopped serrano ham
120 ml / 4 fl oz / ½ cup fino (dry) Montilla or Sherry
4 tablespoons water
Salt and pepper
Sprig of fresh mint, plus additional chopped mint for garnish

Allow the artichokes to defrost or plunge them into boiling water and drain. Crush the saffron in a mortar and add the hot water. Allow to steep.

Heat the oil in a cazuela (earthenware casserole) or frying pan. Add the garlic, onion and ham and sauté 1 minute. Add the artichokes and sauté 5 minutes. Stir in the saffron water, fino Montilla, water, salt, pepper and sprig of mint. Cover and cook until artichokes are tender, 15 minutes.

Serve hot sprinkled with chopped fresh mint.

■ ARTICHOKE HOW-TO

Cut a slice off the artichoke bottom, discarding stem. Pull away and discard two layers of tough outer leaves. Lay the artichoke on a cutting board and cut through it about one-third up from the bottom. (A serrated knife works well.) Discard upper leaves. Cut the remaining bottom in quarters. If the artichokes are very large, use a knife tip to cut out and discard the fuzzy "choke". Small ones can be cooked, choke and all. Add cut artichokes directly to the pan. Or, if cutting them up in advance of cooking, rub all the cut surfaces with a slice of lemon and place the prepared artichoke bottoms in a bowl of water to which you have added a squeeze of lemon. This keeps the cut surfaces from turning dark.

Bring a pan of salted water to the boil and add the cut-up artichokes. If the artichokes are to cook further in the Córdoba wine sauce, blanch them for 5 minutes and drain. If you intend to serve them cold, cook them until tender and a leaf easily pulls away, about 15 minutes. Drain.

You will need 16 to 20 trimmed artichokes to prepare the recipe for Artichokes with Ham and Córdoba Wine.

Espinacas con Garbanzos
SPINACH WITH CHICKPEAS

Some of the best tapas were invented to use leftovers. This tapa, popular in Sevilla tascas, makes use of cooked chickpeas from the grand midday *cocido*, boiled dinner. In this recipe, you start with chickpeas from a jar or tin instead of the stew pot.

Makes 8 tapas or 4 main dishes.

350 g / 12 ounces washed and chopped
   spinach
3 tablespoons olive oil
½ onion, chopped
1 tomato, peeled, seeded, and chopped
2 (570-g / 20-oz) jars chickpeas
⅛ teaspoon saffron threads

2 cloves garlic, coarsely chopped
½ teaspoon coarse salt
Freshly ground black pepper
2 teaspoons pimentón (paprika)
¼ teaspoon ground cumin
120 ml / 4 fl oz / ½ cup) water
2 tablespoons wine vinegar

Place the spinach in a pot with a little water. Bring to the boil and cook until spinach is wilted. Drain and reserve.

Heat the oil in a deep frying pan or earthenware cazuela. Sauté the onion until softened, 3 minutes. Add the tomato and sauté 2 minutes.

Crush the saffron in a mortar. Add the garlic and salt and grind the garlic to a paste. (This can also be done in a blender.) Add the pepper, pimentón and cumin. Stir the water into the paste. Add the spice mixture to the pan. Add the chickpeas without draining. Add the spinach and vinegar. Bring to the boil then reduce heat.

Cover the pan and simmer the chickpeas 15 minutes. Serve hot.

Habas Salteadas con Jamón
BROAD BEANS SAUTÉED WITH HAM

This is a specialty in the tapa bars of Granada. Fresh broad beans (fava beans) come into the market in the springtime, but this tasty dish can be made year-round with frozen beans. Use the tiny "baby" beans, if possible. Sometimes the beans are divided between individual cazuelitas, each topped with an egg, then baked until the eggs are just set. This makes a fine luncheon dish.

Makes 8 tapas or 4 starters.

4 tablespoons olive oil
1 onion, chopped
3 cloves chopped garlic
90 g / 3 oz serrano ham, chopped
2 (400-g / 14-oz) packets frozen broad (fava) beans
2 teaspoons flour
300 ml / ½ pint (1 ¼ cup) water
1 teaspoon salt
Freshly ground black pepper
1 tablespoon chopped parsley plus additional to serve

Heat the oil in a cazuela (earthenware casserole) or heavy enamelled casserole. Sauté the onion and garlic until softened, 5 minutes. Add the ham and sauté 2 minutes. Stir in the beans and sauté 3 minutes. Sprinkle with the flour and stir.

Add water, salt, pepper and parsley. Bring to the boil, cover, and simmer until beans are tender, 15 to 20 minutes for small ones. Sprinkle with additional chopped parsley to serve.

Champiñones al Ajillo
MUSHROOMS SAUTÉED WITH GARLIC

Some tapa bars specialise in *setas*, seasonal wild mushrooms—chanterelles, boletus and more. This recipe can be adapted to wild mushrooms, but the timing will differ depending on the variety. For instance, boletus give out a lot of water and need longer sautéing than cultivated white mushrooms. The mushrooms make a great side dish with steak.

Makes 6 tapas or side dishes.

900 g / 2 lb mushrooms
6 tablespoons olive oil
6 cloves garlic, sliced crosswise
60 g / 2 oz chopped bacon or serrano ham
Red chilli flakes (optional)
1 teaspoon salt
120 ml / 4 fl oz / ½ cup dry Sherry
½ cup chopped flat-leaf parsley

Clean the mushrooms in running water and pat them dry. If they are large, cut them in half through the stems, then slice them thickly. Small mushrooms can be quartered.

Heat the oil in a large frying pan. Add the garlic, bacon or ham and chilli and sauté 2 minutes. Add the mushrooms and continue sautéing, about 6 minutes. Add the salt and Sherry and cook 6 minutes longer. Stir in the parsley. Serve the mushrooms hot.

Pisto
VEGETABLE MEDLEY

You say, toe-mah-toe, I say, toe-may-toe. You say, *ratatouille*, they say, *pisto*. This is, essentially, the very same dish—and, by the way, it was probably Spanish before it was French. Never mind—it's a splendid vegetable dish. Serve it as a juicy side dish alongside potato tortilla, as a sauce for any of the fried foods, as a starter or, topped with a fried egg, as a luncheon dish.

Makes 8 tapas or 6 side dishes.

680 g / 1 ½ lb aubergine (eggplant),
    peeled and cut in 25-mm /1-in cubes
Salt
3 tablespoons olive oil
1 onion, chopped
2 cloves garlic, chopped
1 green bell pepper, cut in squares
600 g / 1 lb 5 oz tomatoes, peeled,
    seeded and chopped

450 g / 1 lb courgette (zucchini),
    cut in 25-mm / 1-in cubes
1 teaspoon salt
½ teaspoon crumbled dry oregano
½ teaspoon pimentón (paprika)
Freshly ground black pepper
Chopped parsley
Vinegar (optional)

Place the cubed aubergine in a colander and sprinkle it liberally with salt. Let it drain for 1 hour.

In a pan, heat the oil and sauté the onion and aubergine for 5 minutes. Add the garlic and green pepper and sauté another minute, then add the tomatoes and courgette. Sauté on a medium heat another 5 minutes.

Season with salt, oregano, pimentón and pepper. Cover and cook on a slow heat until vegetables are soft, about 20 minutes, stirring frequently so vegetables don't scorch. The mixture should be juicy, but not soupy.

Serve hot or cold, garnished with chopped parsley. If serving cold, add a touch of vinegar.

Patatas a lo Pobre
POTATO CASSEROLE

The Spanish name means "poor guy potatoes," because it's a meatless dish. Serve it as a vegetarian tapa or as a side dish with roast meat or fish.

Makes 10 tapas or side dishes.

150 ml / ¼ pint / ⅔ cup olive oil
2 kg / 4 ¼ lb baking potatoes, peeled and sliced 6 mm / ¼ in thick
2 onions, sliced
1 green bell pepper, cut in strips
1 tomato, quartered and sliced
3 cloves garlic, chopped
3 tablespoons chopped parsley
2 bay leaves
½ teaspoon thyme
1 teaspoon pimentón (paprika)
100 ml / 3 ½ fl oz / ⅓ cup white wine
100 ml / 3 ½ fl oz / ⅓ cup boiling water
Salt and pepper

Preheat oven to 180ºC / 350ºF.

Pour a little of the oil into the bottom of a cazuela (earthenware casserole) or oven-safe pan. Arrange alternating layers of potatoes, onions, green peppers and tomato slices, sprinkling each layer with some of the chopped garlic and parsley. Break the bay leaves into pieces and tuck them among the potatoes with the thyme. Sprinkle with the pimentón and pour over the remaining oil.

Add the wine and water. Season with salt and pepper. Cover the casserole with foil and put it in the oven. Bake until potatoes are tender, about 60 minutes. Let the casserole rest 10 minutes before serving.

Patatas a la Riojana
POTATOES, LA RIOJA STYLE

Should you be *de tapeo* in the neighbourhood of Calle de Laurel in Logroño, capital of La Rioja, you should sample this great potato dish. It's the perfect foil for a robust Rioja *crianza*, a red with a little ageing time.

Makes 8 tapas or 4 starters.

1 ½ kg / 3 ½ lb mature baking potatoes
4 tablespoons olive oil
1 onion, chopped
1 small green bell pepper, chopped
1 teaspoon pimentón
1 bay leaf
1 teaspoon salt
450 ml / ¾ pint / 2 cups water
340 g /12 oz soft chorizo, cut in 8 pieces

Peel the potatoes and cut them into 4-cm / 1 ½ -inch chunks.

Heat the oil in a cazuela (earthenware casserole) and sauté the onion until softened, about 5 minutes. Add the potatoes and turn them in the oil for another 5 minutes. Add the green pepper, pimentón, bay leaf, salt and water. Bring to the boil, simmer potatoes for 10 minutes.

Add the chorizo to the potatoes and continue to cook for another 25 minutes, or until the potatoes are tender.

Let the dish rest for 10 minutes before serving. The cooking liquid should be thickened to a sauce consistency.

Patatas a la Importancia
POTATOES WITH IMPORTANCE

These are potatoes "putting on airs," a fancy way to prepare a plebeian, vegetarian dish. In traditional cooking, this would be a main dish for a family meal. In trendy tapa bars, it's paired with "important" ingredients such as caramelised goose liver, truffles, or lobster. If you don't have saffron, substitute a spoonful of pimentón (paprika), for colour and flavour.

Makes 8 tapas, 6 side dishes or 4 main dishes.

1 kg / 2 ¼ lb baking potatoes (about 4 large)
65 g / 2 ¼ oz / ½ cup plus additional 1 tablespoon plain flour
Salt
2 eggs, beaten with 1 teaspoon of water
240 ml / 8 fl oz / 1 cup olive oil
Pinch of saffron
4 tablespoons hot water
1 small onion, finely chopped
½ cup flat-leaf parsley plus additional to serve
3 cloves garlic
Freshly ground black pepper
120 ml / 4 fl oz / ½ cup white wine
300 ml / ½ pint / 1 ¼ cup water or chicken stock

Peel the potatoes and cut them crosswise into 10-mm / ⅜ -in slices. Place the sliced potatoes in a large plastic bag with flour and ½ teaspoon salt. Tie the bag securely and shake the potatoes with the flour until they are well coated. Discard the bag and any excess flour.

Place the beaten eggs in a shallow bowl. Heat the oil in a large frying pan. Dip the floured slices of potato into the beaten egg, then fry them in the oil, a few at a time, turning once, until browned on both sides, about 4 minutes. The potatoes will not be cooked through. Remove the potatoes as they are browned, draining off the oil, and reserve.

Crush the saffron and place in a small bowl. Pour over hot water and allow to steep.

Place 1 tablespoon of the oil in which the potatoes were fried into a large cazuela (earthenware casserole) or other flameproof casserole. Sauté the onion until softened, but not browned, 5 minutes.

Combine the parsley, garlic, pepper, wine, saffron water, 1 teaspoon salt and additional 1 tablespoon flour in a blender. Add any egg that remained from dipping the potato slices. Blend until smooth. Pour this mixture into the cazuela with the onions. Add the water or stock. Add the potatoes, spreading them evenly.

Cook on high heat until liquid begins to boil, then moderate heat so potatoes bubble gently. Don't stir, but shake the cazuela frequently. When potatoes are tender, about 25 minutes, remove cazuela from heat and allow to set 10 minutes. Garnish with additional parsley and serve immediately.

cazuelitas
SAUCY DISHES

Mejillones a la Marinera
MUSSELS, FISHERMEN'S STYLE

The addition of saffron and cream transforms humble fishermen's-style mussels into a sublime dish. Serve this tapa with crusty bread. To turn it into a main course, serve the mussels with steamed rice, pasta or even mashed potatoes for soaking up the lovely sauce.

Makes 8 tapas; 4 starters, or 2 main dishes.

¼ teaspoon saffron
4 tablespoons hot water
3 tablespoons olive oil
1 tablespoon chopped onion
3 cloves chopped garlic
Pinch of fennel seeds
1 medium tomato, peeled, seeded and chopped
100 ml / 4 fl oz/ ½ cup dry white wine
1 kg / 2 ¼ lb mussels (18 to 24), cleaned
75 ml / 3 fl oz / ⅓ cup cream
Chopped flat-leaf parsley

Crush the saffron in a small bowl. Add the water and allow it to stand.

Heat the oil on medium heat in a deep pan with a lid. Sauté the onion and garlic until softened, 2 minutes. Add the fennel seeds and tomato. Cook on high heat 3 minutes. Add the wine, saffron water and mussels. Cover the pan and cook on a high heat just until mussel shells open, 3 to 6 minutes.

Use a slotted spoon to remove mussels from the pan and place them in a bowl. Discard any which have not opened. When cool enough to handle, remove and discard empty half-shell.

Add the cream to the pan with any liquid in the bowl of mussels. Cook, stirring, 5 minutes. Return the mussels to the pan and heat briefly. Serve hot sprinkled with chopped parsley.

■ MUSSEL BOUND

You don't have to pump iron to get this kind of mussel. Bulging bi-valves can be found at your local fish market. Most mussels come from Galicia in northwest Spain, where they are "farmed" on flats anchored in the Atlantic surf.

Buy mussels with their shells tightly closed. Throw out any that are cracked or open. Cook mussels the same day you buy them. After cooking, they may be kept, with or without shells, tightly covered and refrigerated, for up to two days. One kilo / 2 ¼ pounds provides about 18 large mussels or 24 small ones.

To clean mussels: Use a short, sturdy knife to chip off any barnacles and other encrustations from the shells. The "beard" looks like a tuft of coarse seaweed sticking out from the shell. Pull it down to the mussel's hinge and cut it off with a knife or scissors. Wash the mussels in several changes of water.

Gambas al Ajillo
PRAWNS SIZZLED WITH GARLIC

First you catch a tantalising whiff of garlic. Then, as the cazuelita is set before you, you feel the heat radiating from the little dish. The lid is lifted and the oil spits and splutters. Small pink prawns, golden slices of garlic and deep red flecks of chilli dance in the oil. Now a taste— this is the essence of tapa bar sensory experience.

In tapa bars, the dish is usually prepared to order in small, individual ramekins. You can make it to serve a larger number—though it won't have quite the same sizzle! By the way, the prawns are completely peeled, including the tails. In Andalusia, this tapa is known as *gambas al pil pil*, for the onomatopoeia of spitting oil. Never mind that pil pil in Basque cuisine is something quite different.

Makes 4 tapas.

40 medium-size raw, peeled prawns (shrimp), about 225 g / 8 oz
8 tablespoons olive oil
4 cloves garlic, sliced crosswise
4 slices dried chilli pepper
2 tablespoons water
Pinch of pimentón (paprika)
Pinch of coarse salt
Bread for serving

Rinse the prawns and pat them dry. Heat the oil in a cazuela or heavy frying pan until it is shimmering, but not smoking. Add the garlic and chilli and cook until garlic begins to colour, 30 seconds. Add the prawns in a single layer. Cook them, stirring, until they turn pink, 30 to 40 seconds.

Remove the pan from the heat. Stir in the water. Sprinkle with pimentón and salt. Spoon the prawns, garlic and juices into 4 individual ramekins. Serve with bread.

Pimientos de Piquillo Rellenos con Gambas
PIQUILLO PEPPERS STUFFED WITH PRAWNS

Piquillo peppers are small, triangular-shaped red peppers. They are famous in Navarra, where they are roasted, skinned and tinned. Sweet and slightly piquant piquillos are lovely stuffed with seafood. The classic stuffing is bacalao, salt cod. In this version, which you might find in the taverns of San Sebastian, the filling is prawns in a creamy béchamel sauce.

Makes 6 tapas or 4 starters.

4 tablespoons olive oil

2 tablespoons finely chopped onion

2 cloves garlic, chopped

2 tablespoons plain flour plus additional for
    dredging peppers

1 tablespoon dry Sherry

230 ml / 8 fl oz / 1 cup minus 1 tablespoon milk

½ teaspoon salt

150 g / 5 ¼ oz uncooked, small, peeled prawns
    (shrimp)

2 (185-g / 6 ½ -oz) tins piquillo peppers
    (16 to 20 peppers), drained

4 tablespoons white wine

1 egg, beaten

Olive oil to fry the peppers

50 g / 1 ¾ oz grated cheese

Heat 2 tablespoons of the oil in a saucepan on medium heat. Sauté the onion and 1 clove of the garlic, 2 minutes. Stir in the flour and cook 1 minute. Whisk in the Sherry, milk and salt. Cook, stirring constantly, until sauce is thickened, 5 minutes. Stir in the prawns and cook 2 minutes.

Select 12 of the drained peppers. Spoon prawn filling into them. Place them in a single layer on a shallow pan or tray. When all are filled, cover with plastic wrap and refrigerate for at least 1 hour to allow the mixture to thicken.

While the prawn mixture is chilling, prepare the sauce. Combine remaining 2 tablespoons oil, 1 clove of garlic, white wine and remaining piquillo peppers in a blender and blend until smooth.

Preheat oven to 180ºC / 350ºF.

Place flour and beaten egg in two shallow bowls. Heat oil in a frying pan on medium heat. Dip the open end of the stuffed peppers into flour, then dredge the peppers in flour. Roll in beaten egg and fry until lightly golden. Remove the peppers from the frying pan and place them in a baking dish or individual cazuelitas. Spoon the sauce over the peppers and top with grated cheese.

Bake the peppers until cheese is melted and sauce is bubbly, 15 minutes. Serve hot or room temperature.

Txangurro
CRAB GRATIN

Txangurro is the Basque word for the spider crab. The flaked meat from boiled crabs is added to a savoury sauce spiked with brandy, then returned to the crab shell to gratin. If you haven't got crab shells, use oven-safe ramekins. Meaty fish such as angler (monkfish) can be used in place of crab. This also makes a nice filling for tartlet shells.

Makes 8 tapas or 4 starters.

4 tablespoons olive oil
2 medium onions, chopped
1 carrot, chopped
2 cloves garlic, chopped
1 (780-g / 1 ¾-lb) tin chopped tomatoes
4 tablespoons brandy
120 ml / 4 fl oz / ½ cup dry Sherry
450 g / 1 lb fresh or frozen crab meat, drained and liquid reserved
½ teaspoon hot pimentón (paprika) or pinch of cayenne
½ teaspoon salt
2 tablespoons chopped parsley
1 bay leaf
40 g / 1 ½ oz / 1 cup fresh bread crumbs
1 tablespoon butter

Heat the oil in a deep frying pan and sauté the onion, carrot and garlic for 5 minutes. Add the tomatoes and cook at a high heat 5 minutes more. (You can also add pieces of crab shell.)

Add 3 tablespoons of the brandy, Sherry, 4 tablespoons of liquid drained from the crabs, pimentón, salt, parsley and bay leaf. Bring to the boil, then simmer the sauce for 40 minutes.

Discard the bay leaf. Purée the sauce in a blender, then sieve it. Return the sauce to the pan and stir in the crab meat. Add remaining brandy. Cook 5 minutes.

Preheat oven to 200ºC / 400ºF.

Spoon the mixture into the crab shells or oiled ramekins. Sprinkle the tops with breadcrumbs and dot with butter. Bake until the top is lightly golden, about 20 minutes.

Vieiras Gratinadas
SCALLOP GRATIN

Gratin the scallops in their own shells or put them in small, individual cazuelitas. Scallops are the emblem of Santiago de Compostela in Galicia, so be sure to accompany this tapa with Galicia´s wonderful Albariño white wines from DO Rías Baixas.

Makes 6 tapas or starters.

1 pound fresh or frozen scallops, thawed
1 tablespoon fresh lemon juice
4 tablespoons olive oil
1 onion, finely chopped
1 clove garlic, finely chopped
60 g / 2 oz serrano ham, chopped
4 tablespoons white wine
2 teaspoons pimentón (paprika)
Pinch of hot pimentón or cayenne
2 tablespoons chopped parsley
Salt and pepper
4 tablespoons fine dry bread crumbs

Pat the scallops dry. If they are very large, they can be sliced in half. Place them in a bowl with the lemon juice.

Heat 3 tablespoons of the oil in a frying pan and sauté the onion, garlic and ham on a medium heat until onion is softened, about 15 minutes.

Add the wine and cook until partially reduced. Remove the pan from the heat and stir in the two kinds of pimentón, parsley, salt and pepper.

Divide the scallops between 6 scallop shells or individual ramekins. Put a spoonful of the onion mixture onto each shell. Sprinkle with the bread crumbs. Drizzle the remaining 1 tablespoon of oil over the scallops.

Set the shells or ramekins on a grill pan (broiler pan) and place the pan under the grill (broiler) until scallops are bubbling and tops lightly browned, about 8 minutes.

Almejas con Fabes
CLAMS WITH BEANS

This dish is typical of the *sidrerías*, cider houses, of Asturias in northern Spain..

Makes 8 tapas or 4 starters.

900 g / 2 lb clams, washed in several changes of water
¼ teaspoon saffron, crushed
2 tablespoons hot water
3 tablespoons olive oil
½ onion, chopped
60 g / 2 oz serrano ham, chopped
2 cloves garlic, chopped
1 tablespoon fine, dry bread crumbs
3 (540-g / 1 lb 3-oz) jars cannellini beans
Salt and pepper
Pinch of dried thyme

Scrub the clams and put them in a pan with a very little water. Cover and steam them open over a high heat, shaking the pan until the clam shells open. Remove from heat. Strain the liquid and reserve it. Shell the clams, discarding the shells.

Put the saffron in a small bowl and add the hot water. Allow to steep 10 minutes.

Heat the oil in a cazuela or deep frying pan.

Add the onion and sauté 3 minutes until softened. Add the ham and garlic and sauté 1 minute more. Stir in the bread crumbs and beans with their liquid. Season with salt, pepper and thyme. Add the saffron water. Bring to the boil and reduce to a simmer. Add the clams to the beans. Simmer for 10 minutes. Serve hot.

IN A CLAM SHELL

A happy tapa bar custom is to order plates *para picar*, to share around the table, where everyone dips into the communal dish. One of the best tapas for this is *almejas a la marinera*, clams in a briny, garlicky sauce. You pick up the clams and slurp them right off the shells, then dip chunks of bread into the delicious juices.

Clams come from small to large, wedge-shaped to rounded, ridged to smooth. The big Venus shells with their mahogany-coloured shells are best prised open and eaten raw with just a squeeze of lemon. Cooked, they can be tough. Mid-size and small clams are best steamed open and served immediately. Especially esteemed are tiny, wedge-shelled *coquinas* and plump *almejas del norte*.

At the market, buy clams with tightly-closed shells. Discard any with opened or chipped shells. Commercial clammeries purge the bi-valves of sand before sending them to market. But, clams dug from tidal beaches need to be left in cold, salted water for several hours to get rid of grittiness. Cook clams the same day you buy them. Once cooked, they can be refrigerated, tightly covered, for use another day.

Preparing that tapa bar special, clams

marinera, is ever so easy. Sauté chopped onion and garlic in olive oil in a deep frying pan. You can add flecks of red chilli, if you like. Add white wine and clams. Raise the heat to high. Cover the pan and shake it until clam shells open, 3 to 4 minutes. Pour into a serving dish and top with chopped parsley.

cazuelitas
SAUCY DISHES

Albondiguitas de Pescado
FISH BALLS IN SAUCE

Use any white fish, such as hake, cod, sole, grouper or halibut for these fish balls. Fresh fish is best, but frozen will work just fine. The fish balls are also a good way to use leftover cooked fish. Use about 1 ½ cups flaked, cooked fish and leave off the poaching step.

If you're serving these fish balls for dinner, accompany them with steamed white rice.

Makes about 32 fish balls: 12 to16 tapas, 8 starters or 4 main dishes.

FOR THE FISH BALLS:
450 g / 1 lb boneless, skinless white fish
1 litre / 1 ¾ pints / 4 ¼ cups water
Slice of lemon
Sprigs of parsley
Slice of onion
1 bay leaf
Salt
60 g / 2 oz crustless bread (about 8
    baguette slices)
120 ml / 4 fl oz / ½ cup milk
2 cloves garlic
½ cup chopped parsley
½ teaspoon salt
Grated lemon zest
1 egg
Plain flour for dredging the fish balls
    (about 30 g / 1 oz / ¼ cup)
Olive oil for frying

FOR THE SAUCE:
3 tablespoons olive oil
1 onion, chopped
1 small green pepper, chopped
1 tomato, peeled, seeded and chopped
120 ml / 4 fl oz / ½ cup dry white wine
180 ml / 6 fl oz / ¾ cup reserved fish broth
    or water
Chopped fresh herbs to serve (such as
    parsley, coriander/cilantro or basil)

FOR THE FISH BALLS: Wash the pieces of fish. Place the water in a pan with lemon slice, parsley, onion slice, bay and salt. Bring to the boil and simmer 5 minutes. Add the fish to the pan and simmer just until it flakes easily, about 5 minutes. Lift the fish out with a slotted spoon and allow to cool. Strain and reserve the broth in which the fish was poached.

When fish is cool enough to handle, flake or chop it.

Pour the milk over the bread slices in a small bowl and allow to soak for 10 minutes.

In a food processor finely chop together the garlic and parsley. Squeeze out excess liquid from the bread and process the bread until fairly smooth. Add the salt, lemon zest and egg and process to blend. Add the flaked fish and pulse several times just to combine the fish with the bread mixture. Refrigerate the fish mixture, tightly covered, at least 30 minutes and up to 8 hours.

Place the flour in a shallow pan. Shape the fish mixture into 3-cm / 1 ¼-in balls and place them in the flour. Roll the balls to coat evenly with flour.

Add enough oil to cover the bottom of a large frying pan. Heat the oil and fry the fish balls, in two or three batches, turning them to brown on all sides, about 5 minutes total. Remove them as they are browned.

FOR THE SAUCE: Heat the 3 tablespoons oil in a clean frying pan. Sauté the chopped onion and green pepper on medium heat for 5 minutes. Add the tomato and fry on a high heat until tomato sweats out its liquid, about 5 minutes. Add the wine and reserved strained fish broth. Season with salt and pepper. Bring to the boil, cover and simmer 20 minutes.

Add the fish balls to the sauce and reheat gently, about 6 minutes.

Sprinkle with chopped fresh herbs to serve.

VARIATION: After frying the fish balls, instead of reheating them in the wine-tomato sauce, serve them piping hot with a dipping sauce such as red chilli sauce (page 257).

Albóndigas de Mariscos en Salsa Verde
SHELLFISH BALLS IN GREEN SAUCE

The tapa bar of El Faro in Cádiz serves marble-sized balls of concentrated prawn flavour in a green sauce with cockles. This is an adaptation of that dish. The little shellfish balls are also delicious added to fish soup or bisque.

Makes 70 (12-mm / ½-in) balls: 10 tapas or starters.

FOR THE SHELLFISH BALLS:
250 ml / 8 fl oz / 1 cup milk
1 bay leaf
65 g / 2 ¼ oz / 1 ½ cups day-old bread crumbs
4 tablespoons olive oil
2 tablespoons finely chopped onions
1 teaspoon pimentón (paprika)
250 g / 9 oz peeled prawns (shrimp)
1 tablespoon brandy (optional)
½ teaspoon salt
Pinch of cayenne
3 egg yolks
Flour for shaping the balls
Boiling water or fish stock

FOR THE GREEN SAUCE:
2 (110-g / 4-oz) tins clams or cockles
3 tablespoons olive oil
4 cloves garlic, sliced crosswise
4 tablespoons dry Sherry
2 teaspoons corn flour (cornstarch)
2 tablespoons water plus additional
    for clam liquid
½ cup chopped flat leaf parsley

FOR THE SHELLFISH BALLS: Bring the milk with the bay leaf to the boil in a small saucepan. Discard the bay leaf. Add the bread crumbs and stir to combine. Return the pan to the heat and cook on a low heat, stirring, until the bread is smooth and the consistency of thick mashed potatoes. Spread it on a plate, cover with plastic wrap and chill at least 1 hour.

In a small frying pan heat the oil and sauté the onions on low heat until softened, 5 minutes. Remove from heat and stir in the pimentón. Allow the onions to cool.

In a blender or food processor, combine the onions, prawns, brandy, salt and cayenne. Blend until fairly smooth. Break up the chilled bread and add to the blender and blend until smooth. Beat in the egg yolks one at a time. Chill the mixture, covered, at least 1 hour and up to 24 hours.

Drop a teaspoonful of the prawn mixture onto a lightly floured board. Very lightly roll it into a small ball, 12 mm / ½ in, and place in a large, oiled frying pan. Continue rolling balls with remaining prawn mixture. (It may be necessary to do them in 2 or more batches.)

Pour boiling water or fish stock over the balls and place on a medium heat. Simmer the balls 10 minutes. Do not let them boil. They will bob to the surface as they cook. Use a slotted spoon to lift them out of the water. If serving immediately, place them directly into the sauce. Otherwise, place them in an oiled oven pan, cover with foil and keep warm in a very low oven.

FOR THE GREEN SAUCE: Drain the clams and reserve all the liquid in a measuring jug. Add enough water to the liquid to measure 240 ml / 8 fl oz / 1 cup.

Heat the oil in a frying pan and add the sliced garlic. Sauté just until it begins to turn golden. Remove the pan from the heat and add the Sherry. Stir the corn flour into 2 tablespoons water until smooth. Stir into the pan along with the clam liquid and water. Cook on low heat, stirring constantly, until the sauce thickens, 3 minutes. Add the drained clams and cook another minute. Stir in the parsley.

Add the shellfish balls to the hot sauce and serve immediately.

Chocos con Habas
CUTTLEFISH WITH BROAD BEANS

This is a popular dish in Huelva, Cádiz and Sevilla—cuttlefish and beans stewed slowly together. The version served at the Bar Modesto in Sevilla includes the cuttlefish ink, adding great depth of flavour. Usually, a good fishmonger will cut up the cuttlefish or squid for you. Tell him to save the ink sac. Otherwise, buy a sachet of cuttlefish ink in the frozen-foods section. Cuttlefish is thick and meaty and needs slow simmering. Squid can be substituted—it will cook in half the time.

Frozen or tinned broad beans can be used in this recipe, but it's even better made with fresh beans in the spring. You will need about 1 kg / 2 ¼ lb broad beans in their shells to make 300 g / 10 ½ oz shelled beans.

Makes 8 tapas or 2 main course servings.

700 g / 1 ½ lb cleaned cuttlefish or squid
1 ink sac or sachet
2 tablespoons olive oil
1 large onion, finely chopped
30 g / 1 oz bacon or serrano ham, chopped
1 clove garlic, chopped
1 tablespoon pimentón (paprika)

120 ml / 4 fl oz / ½ cup white wine
3 tablespoons tomato sauce
Salt and pepper
300 g / 10 ½ oz shelled broad beans
  (fava beans)
Chopped fresh coriander (cilantro) or
  mint leaves to serve

Cut the cuttlefish into 25-mm / 1-in chunks. If using ink from the cuttlefish or squid, crush it in a small bowl and add a few spoonfuls of water. Or empty sachet into bowl and dissolve in water.

Heat the oil in a cazuela or frying pan and add the onion, bacon and garlic. Sauté on medium heat until the onions begin to brown, 12 minutes. Remove from heat and stir in the pimentón. Add the wine, tomato sauce, salt and pepper and the pieces of cuttlefish. Cook, covered, until cuttlefish is very tender, about 45 minutes.

While cuttlefish is cooking, blanch the broad beans in boiling water for 3 minutes and drain. Add the broad beans to the cuttlefish and cook, uncovered, until beans are tender, about 20 minutes more. Strain the ink through a fine sieve into the cuttlefish and stir to blend. Simmer 5 minutes more. Serve hot, sprinkled with cilantro or mint.

Magro con Tomate
PORK WITH TOMATO

Tapa bars in Andalusia serve this tomatoey pork stew accompanied by a small heap of chips (fries). Although *magro* means "lean," the dish is best made with a slightly fatty cut from the shoulder, so the meat stays juicy as it slowly cooks. You can turn this into a sandwich by spooning it onto a split roll or into a main course by serving it with rice or pasta.

Makes 8 tapas or 4 main dishes.

500 g / 17 ½ oz pork shoulder, cut in 25-mm / 1-in cubes
3 tablespoons olive oil
1 clove garlic, finely chopped
1 kg / 2 ¼ lb tomatoes, peeled, seeded and chopped
1 teaspoon salt
1 bay leaf
Pinch of cumin seed
Pinch of oregano
Pinch of cayenne

Heat the oil in a deep frying pan and brown the pieces of pork on a moderately high heat. Keep turning them in the oil until they start to brown, about 5 minutes.

Add the garlic, then the tomatoes. Turn up the heat. Add the salt, bay leaf, cumin, oregano and cayenne. When tomatoes are bubbling, turn down to a simmer and cook, stirring frequently, until tomatoes are reduced. Cook until meat is tender and tomatoes are almost syrupy, 25 to 35 minutes, depending on how juicy the tomatoes are. Stir constantly during the last few minutes, so the sauce doesn't burn. Serve hot.

Bocados de Chorizo al Jerez
SAUSAGE BITES IN SHERRY

This sausage is distinctive Spanish chorizo (see page 40), but, after macerating the meat, instead of stuffing it into sausage casings, you shape it into little patties, brown them, then simmer in Sherry for a delectable sauce. For an authentic flavour, use Spanish paprika, smoky pimentón de la Vera (see page 185), for all or part of the paprika called for in the recipe. Have the butcher mince (grind) together the pork belly, shoulder and fat. In Spain, you should be able to get fresh pork fat from ibérico pork to include in the sausage mix. You need to season the sausage meat 24 hours or more before cooking it.

These piquant sausage bites would make a nice addition to a brunch buffet, served alongside scrambled eggs. As a main dish, serve them with rice, noodles or potatoes as an accompaniment.

Makes 8 tapas or 2 main course servings.

TO PREPARE THE SAUSAGE:
400 g / 14 oz pork belly, minced (ground)
500 g / 1 lb 2 oz boneless pork shoulder,
   minced (ground)
100 g / 3 oz fresh pork fat, minced (ground)
6 cloves garlic
4 tablespoons white wine
4 tablespoons water
1 tablespoon salt
2 tablespoons sweet pimentón (paprika)
1 tablespoon hot pimentón (paprika),
   preferably smoked pimentón de la Vera
1 teaspoon dried oregano
½ teaspoon freshly ground black pepper
1/8 teaspoon fennel seeds
Pinch of ground cloves

TO COOK THE SAUSAGE:
1 tablespoon olive oil
1 onion, chopped
1 teaspoon plain flour
175 ml / 6 fl oz / ¾ cup amontillado
   or fino Sherry
4 tablespoons water
1 apple, chopped
Sprig of fresh rosemary

Place the mince in a non-reactive bowl. In a blender combine the garlic, wine, water, salt, two kinds of pimentón, oregano, pepper, fennel and cloves. Add the spice mixture to the meat and knead it in well. Cover the meat tightly and refrigerate 24 to 48 hours.

Roll the sausage mixture into 35-mm / 1 ½-in balls and flatten them slightly, forming 45-mm / 1 ¾-in patties.

Heat the oil in a large heavy frying pan on medium-high heat and brown the patties in batches, 3 to 4 minutes. Remove them when browned on both sides. Drain off the remaining fat and reserve it, discarding the pan drippings.

Place 2 tablespoons of reserved fat in a clean pan. Sauté the onion on medium heat until softened, 4 minutes. Stir in the flour and cook 3 minutes. Add the Sherry and water and stir until liquid begins to simmer. Return the sausage patties to the pan with the apple and rosemary. Cover and simmer 45 minutes. Remove rosemary before serving.

> **TIP:** If sausage mixture is too sticky to roll, dip your hands in cool water before patting it out.

▪ PIMENTÓN—RUDDY GOOD

Pimentón is a ruddy-coloured powder that probably is the favourite spice in Spanish cooking. While, at first glance, you might think it's just paprika, pimentón has some ethnic differences. It's produced both in Murcia, in eastern Spain, and in the La Vera region of Extremadura in western Spain. Pimentón comes from the *capsicum annuum* pepper, the chilli pepper discovered by Columbus on his first trip to the New World. He was looking for the "Indies," the source of "pepper," *pimienta* in Spanish. When he found the hot-tasting capsicum, Columbus called it *pimiento*, from which comes pimentón. And paprika too.

Why not call it paprika? The word "paprika" derives from the Serbo-Croatian word for pepper. And Croatia is much further than Spain is from the source of those peppers. So, just call it pimentón.

In Murcia, in eastern Spain, the hot, dry Mediterranean climate allows the peppers to be sun-dried. But, in autumn when the peppers ripen in La Vera, early rains in the Atlantic climate of Extremadura make sun-drying impossible. So, the peppers are smoke-dried 10 to 15 days over smouldering chunks of wild holm oak. From the smoking sheds they're carried to the milling factory where they are stone-ground to red powder. A brilliant solution! The slow smoking fixes the natural carotenoid pigments of the peppers, producing an intensely red spice. It also adds an ineffable natural smokiness that complements many foods.

Spanish pimentón, whether smoked or unsmoked, comes in three flavours--*dulce*, sweet; *agridulce*, bittersweet, and *picante*, spicy-hot—which are made from three different subspecies of peppers. Sweet pimentón, smoked or unsmoked, is the most versatile, while the bittersweet adds complexity to a dish. The spicy-hot is piquant and flavourful, but not as fiery as cayenne.

Pimentón de la Vera, the only pimentón with a surname, enjoys denominación de origen (DO), a guarantee of quality by the La Vera governing board. Look for DO La Vera labels on tins or packets of the spice.

In Spain, the lion's share of pimentón goes to the sausage-making industry. The most emblematic Spanish sausage, garlicky chorizo, is coloured and flavoured with it.

Pimentón is widely used in home cooking too and not just a sprinkle for colour. Heaping tablespoons of it go into sauces where it provides richness of flavour. In Extremadura, La Vera pimentón is the preferred type. Elsewhere in Spain, unsmoked pimentón is used lavishly, even in paella and other rice dishes.

Substitute Spanish pimentón in any recipe calling for paprika. It gives a little flamenco flounce to Hungarian goulash. Use the La Vera spice, with its earthy, smoky aroma, in barbecue sauces, marinades and spice rubs. The spicy-hot version adds pizzazz to beans and lentils, gratin dishes, seafood cocktail sauces. The hot stuff is a wake-up call for humble devilled eggs or potato salad.

Stir pimentón into a little water and blend it smooth before adding to a sauce. As with paprika, take care not to scorch the pimentón, else it becomes bitter. If using pimentón on barbecued food, add it during the last few minutes of grilling, so that it doesn't burn.

Pollo al Ajillo
CHICKEN SAUTÉED WITH GARLIC

Chicken sautéed with loads of garlic and simmered in Sherry makes one of southern Spain's most appetising tapas. You can turn this tapa bar classic into a main course—instead of cutting the chicken into small pieces, use a jointed chicken and increase cooking time.

Makes 12 tapas or 6 main dishes.

900 g / 2 lb chicken wings (or whole chicken cut into bite-sized pieces)
Salt and pepper
1 head garlic (about 12 cloves)
4 tablespoons olive oil
1 bay leaf
120 ml / 4 fl oz / ½ cup dry or medium-dry Sherry
Chopped parsley

Cut off the wing tips and discard (or save for stock). Divide each wing into two joints. Sprinkle chicken pieces with salt and pepper. Lightly smash the garlic cloves to split the skins, but do not peel them.

Heat the oil in a deep frying pan or cazuela (earthenware casserole). Add the chicken pieces and garlic to the oil and sauté them very slowly.

When chicken is browned on all sides, add the bay leaf and Sherry. Continue cooking until the liquid is cooked away and the chicken begins to sizzle again. Serve hot garnished with chopped parsley.

Riñones al Jerez
KIDNEYS IN SHERRY SAUCE

Some tapa bars specialise in offal, from kidneys to liver, sweetbreads to tongue, brains, testicles, tripe, heart and lungs. One dish that is so good it appears on tapa bar lists everywhere is this one, kidneys braised with Sherry. At Madrid's polished Lhardy, the kidneys are served in *barquitas*, tartlet shells, instead of cazuelitas.

Makes 6 to 8 tapas.

900 g /2 lb veal or lamb kidneys
Milk
4 tablespoons olive oil
½ onion, finely chopped
170 g / 6 oz mushrooms, cleaned and quartered
1 clove garlic, finely chopped
1 ½ tablespoons plain flour

120 ml / 4 fl oz / ½ cup dry Sherry
120 ml / 4 fl oz / ½ cup beef stock or water
½ teaspoon salt
Freshly ground black pepper
1 bay leaf
Chopped parsley

Split the kidneys in quarters, discarding the kernel of fat in the centre. Put the pieces of kidney to soak in milk, covered and refrigerated, for one hour or more. Drain and discard the soaking liquid.

Cut the kidneys into pieces. Veal kidneys are divided by lobes, so it's easy to cut them into pieces of about 35 mm / 1 ½ in square.

Heat the oil in a frying pan and sauté the chopped onion, mushrooms and garlic until onion is softened, about 5 minutes. Turn up the heat to brown them lightly. Then add the pieces of kidney and regulate the heat so they don't brown too fast. Stir and sauté until lightly coloured, about 5 minutes.

Stir in the flour, then add the Sherry and beef stock. Add salt, pepper and bay leaf. Simmer gently, but do not boil, until kidneys are tender, about 60 minutes. Serve sprinkled with chopped parsley.

Albóndigas en Salsa de Almendras
MEATBALLS IN ALMOND SAUCE

Meatballs are favourite tapa bar fare. This version, with a saffron and almond sauce, is especially delicious, but you could also finish the meatballs in tomato sauce (page 239).

Makes about 36 meatballs: 12 tapas or 4 main dishes.

FOR THE MEATBALLS:
340 g / 12 oz minced (ground) beef
340 g / 12 oz minced (ground) pork
2 slices stale bread, crusts removed
1 clove garlic, finely chopped
3 tablespoons finely chopped onion
2 tablespoons chopped parsley
½ teaspoon salt
⅛ teaspoon freshly grated nutmeg
2 eggs, beaten
Flour for dredging meatballs
6 tablespoons olive oil

FOR THE SAUCE:
3 tablespoons olive oil
40 almonds, blanched and skinned
1 slice bread
3 tablespoons olive oil
10 peppercorns
½ teaspoon saffron
1 clove or pinch ground cloves
½ teaspoon salt
175 ml / 6 fl oz / ⅔ cup white wine
240 ml / 8 fl oz / 1 cup chicken or meat stock
Chopped parsley

Combine the beef and pork mince in a bowl. Soak the bread in water or milk to cover until soft. Squeeze it out and add to the meat with the garlic, onion, parsley, salt, nutmeg and egg. Knead well to make a smooth mixture.

Form into 25-mm / 1-in balls and roll them in flour. Heat the oil in a large frying pan and fry the meatballs until browned on all sides. Remove and drain.

Place 3 tablespoons of oil in a clean frying pan and fry the almonds, bread and garlic until golden. Remove. Set aside a few almonds for garnish.

In a mortar, crush the peppercorns, saffron, clove and salt. In a food processor or blender, grind together the toasted almonds, bread and garlic with the wine to make a smooth paste. Add the spices to this mixture.

Stir the almond mixture into the oil in the frying pan and add the stock. Bring to the boil, then add the fried meatballs. Simmer the meatballs for 20 minutes in the sauce, adding a little additional liquid if needed.

Serve the meatballs garnished with the reserved toasted almonds and chopped parsley.

SENSUOUS SAFFRON

Saffron is the sensuous spice with its golden-yellow colour, fragrant, floral scent and subtly bittersweet and aromatic taste. It's an essential ingredient in paella rice and many other dishes in Spanish cuisine.

Saffron, the spice, consists of the dried stigmas of a small, mauve-coloured, autumn-blooming crocus, *crocus sativus*. The plant, which originated in the Middle East, was introduced into Spain during the Moorish domination. It has been grown in Spain's central La Mancha region ever since. (Look for *azafrán*, saffron, with the La Mancha DO, designation of origin.)

Saffron is, by definition, an expensive product. That's because it takes the stigmas of approximately 70,000 crocuses to make 450 grams / 1 pound of the spice. Cheap saffron may be adulterated or artificially coloured.

Saffron threads—the dried stigmas— are deep-orange coloured. Pulverize them in a mortar or in a teacup, using the butt end of a knife. Mix the powdered saffron in a small quantity of hot liquid—water, stock or milk, depending on the recipe—and allow to steep for 10 to 20 minutes before stirring it into rice or sauce. This allows the full colour and flavour to be extracted from the spice.

Besides paella, saffron goes into a traditional sauce made with crushed almonds, vegetable and potato dishes, fritter batter and seafood soups. Saffron ice cream and puddings show the sweet side of the spice.

Arroz Negro con Mariscos
BLACK RICE WITH SHELLFISH

Black is beautiful. Squid ink colours and flavours this Catalan rice dish. You have to start with fresh squid, not frozen, to obtain the tiny ink sac. Otherwise, buy sachets of squid ink from the fishmonger or in the frozen foods section of your supermarket.

Makes 8 tapas, 6 starters or 4 main dishes.

12 mussels, scrubbed and steamed open, liquid reserved
900 ml / 1 ½ pints / 4 cups fish stock
1 fresh squid (340 g / 12 oz), cleaned, ink sac reserved
230 g / 8 oz angler fish (monkfish) fillets
4 tablespoons olive oil
8 unpeeled prawns (shrimp)
1 onion, chopped
2 cloves chopped garlic
1 large tomato, peeled, seeded and chopped
2 teaspoons pimentón (paprika)
370 g / 13 oz / 2 cups Spanish medium-short grain rice
Salt and pepper
Garlic mayonnaise (page 248), to serve

> **VARIATION:** Substitute clams for the mussels in the recipe. Steam them open and strain the liquid to add to the rice.

Discard empty half shells from the mussels. Set aside the mussels. Strain the liquid and add it to the fish stock. Place the fish stock in a pan ready to be heated.

Put the ink sac from the squid in a small bowl and add 4 tablespoons of the fish stock to it. Mash the ink sac to release the ink. Set aside.

Cut the cleaned squid into rings or squares.

Cut the angler fish into 4-cm / 1 ½-in pieces.

Heat the oil in a 30-cm / 12-in cazuela or pan until quite hot. Sauté the prawns, about 2 minutes per side, until they are pink and slightly curled. Remove the prawns and reserve them.

Add the cut-up squid to the oil and sauté for 2 minutes. Add the onion and garlic and

continued >

> **Black Rice, continued**

continue cooking on a high heat.

Add the pieces of angler fish and cook another minute on a high heat. Stir in the tomato and pimentón. Continue cooking 5 minutes more.

Bring the reserved fish stock to the boil.

Stir the rice into the cazuela and cook 1 minute. Stir in 900 ml / 1 ½ pints / 4 cups of boiling fish stock. Cook 5 minutes on a high heat.

Use a small sieve to strain the ink mixture into the rice. Stir to mix it well. Lower the heat and cook the rice 5 minutes more. Arrange the cooked mussels and prawns on top of the rice. Don't stir it again. Cook 10 minutes more.

Remove from heat and allow to rest 10 minutes. The rice will continue to cook from the heat of the cazuela. Serve hot, accompanied by the garlic mayonnaise.

■ SQUID HOW-TO

The squid's body is a slender pouch from which protrudes a head with short tentacles. Grasp the head and pull gently. It will come away from the body pouch bringing the innards with it. The ink is enclosed in a tiny silvery sac on the innards. If the ink is required for your recipe, cut the ink sac free without breaking and reserve it in a small bowl. Still inside the body pouch is the quill or cartilage, which looks like a strip of transparent plastic. Grasp the top of it and pull; it will come away in one piece.

Discard it. Cut off the tentacles just above the eyes. Save the tentacles. Discard the remaining head with innards still attached. Rinse out the pouch and pull off the purplish outer skin. The wing flaps will come off too. Save them. The cleaned squid consists of tentacles, two wing flaps and a body pouch. Use kitchen scissors to cut the pouch crosswise into rings or slit it lengthwise and cut into squares. If using the ink, mash the ink sac, add some white wine or stock, then sieve it before adding to the sauce.

Estofado de Rabo de Toro
OXTAIL STEW

This lusty stew, traditionally made with bull's tail from a bullfight, requires long, slow cooking. Dished out into individual cazuelitas and garnished with a few chips (fries), it's favourite tapa bar fare. You could make it with beef chuck or *osso buco* (shank) in place of the oxtail.

Makes 8 tapas or 4 main dishes.

1 whole oxtail (about 1200 g / 2 lb 10 oz), cut crosswise into 8-cm / 3-in segments
3 tablespoons olive oil
1 onion, chopped
1 leek, chopped
3 carrots, diced
2 cloves garlic, chopped
4 slices bacon, chopped
5 tablespoons brandy
120 ml / 4 fl oz / ½ cup water or beef stock

120 ml / 4 fl oz / ½ cup red wine
1 tomato, peeled and chopped
1 bay leaf
Sprig of parsley
Sprig of thyme
Salt and freshly ground black pepper
Red chilli flakes, to taste
Pinch of ground cloves
Chopped parsley, to serve

Wash the pieces of oxtail very well, then blanch them in boiling water for 5 minutes and drain.

In a large pan or cazuela (earthenware casserole), heat the oil and add the onion, leek, carrots, garlic and bacon. Sauté until the onion is soft.

Add the pieces of oxtail and brown them on a medium-high heat. Add the brandy, set it alight, and stir until the flames die down.

Then add the water, wine, tomato, herbs, salt, pepper, red chilli flakes and cloves. Cover and simmer until the meat is very tender, about two hours. Add additional liquid as needed. The sauce should be fairly reduced.

Allow to cool. Strip all the meat from the bones, cut it in bite-size chunks and return it to the sauce. Reheat before serving.

Serve hot, sprinkled with chopped parsley.

Cazuela de Arroz con Mariscos a la Sevillana
RICE AND SEAFOOD, SEVILLA STYLE

Here's a rice dish similar to paella, but, cooked in an earthenware casserole instead of a flat paella pan, the rice comes out juicier than dry paella rice. The flavourful stock, made from prawn shells and fish trimmings, is essential to this rice dish. You can prepare the stock a day in advance. For a luxury version, use chunks of lobster in place of the angler fish (and add the lobster shells to the stock mix). You can use angler fish fillets, but should you be starting out with a whole angler fish, after filleting, use the head, bones and trimmings for the stock too.

Makes 12 tapas or 6 main dishes.

500 g / 1 lb 1 ½ oz unshelled king prawns (jumbo shrimp)

1 bay leaf

Pinch of thyme

Slice of lemon

Salt

2 litres water

½ teaspoon saffron, crushed

2 tablespoons hot water

1 teaspoon pimentón (paprika)

140 ml / ¼ pint / ½ cup+1 tablespoon olive oil

½ onion, chopped

2 thin frying peppers or 1 small green bell pepper, cut in squares

2 cloves garlic, chopped

1 squid (200 g / 7 oz), cleaned and cut into rings

2 medium tomatoes (350 g / 12 oz), peeled, seeded and chopped

400 g / 14 oz / 2 cups medium-short grain rice

85 g / 3 oz / ½ cup fresh or frozen shelled peas

450 g / 1 lb angler fish (monkfish) fillets, cut into 3-cm / 1 ¼-in chunks

150 g / 5 ¼ oz small clams (optional)

3 tablespoons chopped parsley

1 tinned red pimiento

Lemon slices, to serve

Set aside 6 whole, unshelled prawns. Peel all the rest, removing the heads. (Refrigerate the unshelled and the peeled prawns.) Place the prawn shells and heads in a pan and add the bay, thyme, lemon, 1 teaspoon salt and 2 litres of water. Add any fish trimmings, if available. Bring to the boil, reduce heat to a simmer and cook, covered, 40 minutes. Strain and reserve the stock. Discard prawn shells and fish trimmings.

Measure 1150 ml / 2 pints / 5 cups of the reserved stock into a saucepan. Keep it on a low heat, without letting it boil.

Combine the crushed saffron with 2 tablespoons hot water and stir. Allow to steep 5 minutes, then stir in the pimentón until smooth.

Heat the oil in a cazuela (earthenware casserole) or large, deep frying pan over medium heat. Sauté the 6 whole, unpeeled prawns, about 1 minute per side. Remove them and set aside.

Add the onion, peppers and garlic to the oil. Sauté for 3 minutes. Add the squid and continue sautéing, 5 minutes. Add the tomatoes and fry 3 minutes.

Stir in the rice and cook 1 minute. Add the hot stock and the saffron water. Bring to the boil and cook on a brisk fire for 5 minutes. Add salt to taste. (If stock was salted, additional salt may not be needed.)

Stir in the peas, chunks of angler and clams, if using. When liquid begins to bubble again, reduce heat so it just simmers. Cook 5 minutes. Stir in the peeled prawns and parsley. Arrange the sautéed whole prawns on top. Cook 5 minutes more. Garnish with strips of red pimiento. Remove from heat and allow to stand 10 minutes before serving. Serve with lemon slices.

■ RICE HOW-TO

Spanish rice, for paella and other rice dishes, is always a round, medium-short variety that absorbs the flavours with which it cooks. Don't wash the rice. Don't stir it while it's cooking. Start it off at high heat and gradually reduce the flame. Be sure to allow rice time to stand, 10 minutes or longer, after it's removed from the heat.

Fritos

FROM THE FRYING PAN

Fritos
FROM THE FRYING PAN

Fried Almonds (*Almendras Fritas*)

Potato "Bombs" with Meat Filling (*Bomba de Patatas*)

Ham Croquettes (*Croquetas de Jamón*)

Cheese Puffs (*Buñuelos de Queso*)

Fried Goat's Cheese (*Queso Frito*)

Fried Pasties with Tuna Filling (*Empanadillas de Atún*)

Crispy Bites of Marinated Fish (*Bienmesabe*)

Fried Squid Rings (*Calamares Fritos*)

Stuffed Mussels (*Tigres*)

Prawns in Mackintosh (Batter-Fried)
(*Gambas en Gabardinas*)

Batter-Fried Fish Fingers (*Pavías de Merluza*)

Aubergine and Prawn Rollups
(*Rollitos de Berenjena y Langostinos*)

Shrimp Fritters (*Tortillitas de Camarones*)

Cod Fritters with Molasses
(*Tortillitas de Bacalao con Miel de Caña*)

Spinach Fritters (*Tortillitas de Espinacas*)

Fried Chicken Wings (*Alas de Pollo Empanadas*)

Crisp Fried Pork Rolls (*Flamenquines de Cerdo*)

Fried Ham and Cheese Sandwiches *(Emparedados de Jamón y Queso)*

Fried Potatoes with Hot Sauce (*Patatas Bravas*)

Stuffed Chard Stems *(Pencas de Acelgas Rellenas)*

Fried Padrón Peppers *(Pimientos de Padrón)*

"Land Fish" (Fried Aubergine) *(Pez de Tierra)*

"Field Anchovies" (Green Beans) *(Boquerones del Campo)*

"Garden Crayfish" (Asparagus) *(Langostinos de la Huerta)*

fritos
FROM THE FRYING PAN

Golden-brown and crispy on the outside, meltingly soft on the inside and packed with flavour, a good croquette is a joy to bite into. Indeed, croquettes and their fellow fried foods are the irresistible stars of many tapa bars. They appeal to all the senses, go with every drink. Genuine crowd pleasers, fried foods are worth adding to your tapas repertory.

Spain being the great land of olive oil, it comes as no surprise to find fried foods topping the tapas lists. Although, because olive oil is expensive, truth be told, many cooks use cheaper vegetable oils. Perhaps this is false economy, as foods fried in olive oil absorb less oil than those fried in other oils. That means the oil lasts longer and the food is less greasy. Another advantage: olive oil used for frying can be strained and reused four or five times, whereas other oils begin to break down and really shouldn't be used more than twice. Best of all, olive oil imparts authentic Spanish flavour.

Don't use your delicate Arbequina oil for frying. Best are extra virgin oils from Andalusia made from the very stable Picual olive. (For more about olive oil, please see the chapter on Sauces, Dressings, Dips and Spreads.) If cost is an issue, use non-virgin oil (labelled simply "olive oil").

You can fry croquettes or other foods in either a deep-fat fryer or a frying pan.

The advantages of using an electric deep-fat fryer are three: the oil temperature is thermostatically controlled; the large quantity of oil helps maintain the temperature so the food fries evenly, and the basket is helpful for removing the foods.

That said, you don't need special equipment to prepare fried foods at home. A deep frying pan with sloping sides works fine. Pour in oil to a depth of at least 2.5 centimetres / 1 inch. Fry food in small batches, without crowding, and allow the oil to return to frying temperature before adding a new batch.

Heat olive oil to a temperature of 180ºC / 360ºF. The oil will be shimmering, not smoking. At this temperature a crust forms around the food so the oil doesn't penetrate, but it doesn't brown too quickly, allowing the interior of the food to cook thoroughly.

Have ready a platter lined with paper towels. Skim food out of the oil and allow it to drain a few minutes. Cool the oil after use, strain it and store in a dark place for using again.

While fried foods are best straight out of the frying pan, many of them can be prepared—shaped, floured or battered—well in advance. Some even can be fried in advance, then reheated briefly in a hot oven immediately before serving.

Almendras Fritas
FRIED ALMONDS

These fried and spiced almonds are unbelievably delicious. You can use skinned or unskinned almonds. Just take care not to let them get too brown.

Makes 225 g / 8 oz almonds.

225 g / 8 oz / 2 cups almonds
2 tablespoons olive oil
1 teaspoon salt
Pinch of ground cumin
¼ teaspoon pimentón (paprika)
Pinch of cayenne

Heat the oil in a large frying pan and add the almonds. Fry them, stirring constantly over a medium heat, until they are toasted and very lightly browned, about 1 minute. Remove from heat and immediately sprinkle with salt, cumin, pimentón and cayenne. Cool before serving.

Bomba de Patatas
POTATO "BOMBS" WITH MEAT FILLING

This is a favourite at Málaga tapa bars, where the "bombs" can vary from golf-ball to tennis-ball size. Make the filling very spicy, so these bombs really explode with flavour. Serve them with *alioli*, garlic mayonnaise, (page 248) or with a side of *pisto*, a vegetable medley (page 163). For the meat filling, use half pork and half beef.

Makes 15 tapas.

1 kg / 2 ¼ lb potatoes, peeled and cut up
2 teaspoons salt
2 tablespoons olive oil
250 g / 9 oz mince (ground) meat
½ onion, chopped
1 small green pepper, chopped
1 clove garlic, chopped
150 g / 5 oz / ½ cup chopped tomatoes, tinned or fresh

½ teaspoon salt
½ teaspoon cumin
½ teaspoon oregano
½ teaspoon hot pimentón (paprika) or pinch cayenne
1 egg, beaten
125 g / 4 ½ oz / 1 cup fine dry breadcrumbs
Olive oil for frying

Cook the potatoes in boiling water until tender. Drain and mash, adding salt.

In a frying pan, heat the oil and brown the minced meat, 5 minutes. Add the onion, pepper and garlic and continue frying. Add the tomatoes and cook 5 minutes. Season with salt, cumin, oregano and pimentón. Cook, uncovered, until liquid is reduced, about 15 minutes.

Using 2 spoons, shape potatoes into egg-sized balls—5 cm / 2 in—(each about 50 g / 1 ¾ oz). Cut each potato ball in half, make an indentation and fill with a spoonful of the meat filling. Press the halves together and pinch the edges together to seal in the filling.

Dip the potato balls in beaten egg, then roll them in breadcrumbs. Heat oil to a depth of 25 mm / 1 in until hot, but not smoking, and fry the balls, turning until golden, 4 to 5 minutes.

Drain on absorbent towels and serve hot or room temperature.

Do ahead: Shape the potato balls, dip them in egg and breadcrumbs. Place them in a single layer on a tin and freeze. When the balls are frozen, pack them into plastic bags or freezer containers. Completely thaw the potato balls before frying them.

Croquetas de Jamón
HAM CROQUETTES

While they require last-minute frying, croquettes can be shaped and breaded well in advance. In fact, they can even be prepared and frozen. Do not thaw before frying them.

Makes approximately 50 croquettes.

1 litre / 1 ¾ pints / 4 ¼ cups milk
140 ml / ¼ pint / ½ cup+1 tablespoon olive oil
125 g / 4 ½ oz serrano or ibérico ham, chopped
4 tablespoons chopped spring onion,
    including some of green
Pinch of thyme

110 g / 4 oz / 1 cup plain flour, sifted
1 teaspoon salt
Freshly ground black pepper
200 g / 7 oz / 1 ⅔ cups fine dry bread crumbs
3 eggs beaten with 2 teaspoons water
Olive oil for frying

Bring the milk to the boil and set aside. Heat the oil in a pan and sauté the ham gently for 2 minutes without letting it brown. Pour the oil through a sieve into a heat-proof bowl, reserving the ham.

Return the oil to the pan and sauté the onion without letting it brown, 2 minutes. Add the thyme and stir in the flour. Cook 2 minutes without browning the flour. Whisk in the hot milk, stirring hard as the mixture thickens. Cook on low heat, stirring constantly, until the mixture is thick and smooth, 7 minutes. Remove from heat and stir in the ham, salt and pepper.

Spread the mixture in a large, shallow tin that has been lightly oiled. Cover with plastic wrap and allow to cool, then refrigerate at least 2 hours and up to 24 hours.

Place the bread crumbs in another shallow tin. Place the beaten eggs in a shallow bowl. Working with part of the croquette mixture at a time (return the tin to the refrigerator), drop spoonfuls into the tray of breadcrumbs. Roll them in the crumbs to form 5-cm / 2 ½-in cylinders. (Use about 22 g / ¾ oz of the mixture for each croquette.)

Use 2 forks to dip each croquette in beaten egg, letting excess egg drip off, then roll the croquettes again in the crumbs. Take care to completely coat the croquettes so that filling doesn't leak out in the hot oil. As they are shaped and breaded, place them on a tray. Allow to dry for at least 30 minutes.

Place oil in a deep fryer or in a deep frying pan to a depth of at least 25 mm / 1 in. Heat to 180ºC / 360ºF. Fry the croquettes in batches until they are golden-brown, about 3 minutes. Drain on paper towels. Serve hot.

Buñuelos de Queso
CHEESE PUFFS

These are gorgeous, so serve them for special occasions, accompanied by bubbly cava. Vary the flavour by choosing different cheeses. Manchego is excellent, but smoked Idiazábal will give the puffs a different dimension. These are good served with a dipping sauce, such as quince sauce (page 241) or piquillo red pepper sauce (page 251).

Makes about 45 puffs.

250 ml / 9 fl oz / 1 cup+1 tablespoon water
½ teaspoon salt
Pinch of thyme
Pinch of cayenne
80 ml / 3 fl oz / ⅓ cup olive oil

110 g / 4 oz / 1 cup plain flour
4 eggs
125 g / 4 ¼ oz / 2 cups grated cheese
Olive oil for deep frying

Place the water, salt, thyme, cayenne and oil in a pan. Bring to the boil. Lower the heat and add the flour all at once, stirring hard with a wooden spoon until the mixture thickens and pulls away from the sides of the pan. Remove from heat and allow to stand 2 minutes.

Beat in the eggs, one at a time. Thoroughly mix in one egg before adding the next. Stir in the grated cheese.

Place oil in a deep frying pan to a depth of 25 mm / 1 in and heat it until shimmering, 180°C / 360°F. Dip two teaspoons in oil. Scoop up batter with one spoon and use the other to push the batter into the hot oil. Don't crowd the pan. Puffs will bob to the surface. Carefully turn them so they brown on both sides.

Remove when golden, 2 to 3 minutes, and drain on paper towels. Serve immediately.

Do ahead: The cheese puffs can be fried up to four hours before serving. Reheat them in a preheated oven, 195°C / 375°F, for 5 minutes. The puffs can be fried and frozen. Thaw them completely on paper towels before reheating in preheated oven.

VARIATION: Bake the cheese puffs instead of frying them. Line an oven tin with baking parchment. Drop spoonfuls of the batter at least 25 mm / 1 in apart. Bake in preheated oven, 195°C / 375°F, until golden, 30 minutes.

Queso Frito
FRIED GOAT'S CHEESE

This makes a lovely starter—soft, mild cheese with a crisp, breaded coating, served atop salad leaves with toasted pine nuts and a sweet-sour quince sauce. Several kinds of goat's cheese are to be found in Spain. A creamy tangy one, much like French *chèvre*, comes in a roll. The most common, *queso fresco*, is a pure white fresh cheese that can be cut from a round cheese in rectangular or wedge-shaped slices. Cured goat's cheese, which is firmer, will work too, but it doesn't have the dreamy texture of the soft cheese.

Makes 10 tapas or starters.

400 g / 14 oz goat's cheese
Flour for dredging
1 egg, beaten with 1 teaspoon water
100 g / 3 ½ oz / 1 cup fine, dry bread crumbs
Pinch of whole cumin seed

Olive oil for frying (about 80 ml / 3 fl oz / ⅓ cup)
30 g / 1 oz pine nuts
Salad greens, to serve
Thinly sliced apple, to serve
Quince sauce (page 241), to serve

Slice the cheese 10 mm / ⅜ in thick, making about 10 slices that are more or less the same size.

Put the flour and egg in two shallow bowls. Place the bread crumbs in a shallow tin and add the cumin seed. Dredge the cheese slices in flour and pat off excess. Dip them in beaten egg, then coat in breadcrumbs.

Place 1 teaspoon of the oil in a small frying pan and toast the pine nuts until they are golden. Remove.

Place remaining oil in a large frying pan and place over medium heat. Fry the cheese slices until golden brown, about 1 minute per side. Drain on paper towels.

Place greens on salad plates. Top each serving with a slice of fried cheese. Garnish with sliced apple and a scattering of pine nuts. Drizzle the quince sauce over the cheese. Serve immediately, while cheese is still warm.

Empanadillas de Atún
FRIED PASTIES WITH TUNA FILLING

These tiny fried pies will fly off the platters. They can be prepared in advance and frozen, then fried shortly before serving.

Makes 40 (85 mm / 3 ½ in) pasties.

FOR THE DOUGH:
250 g / 8 ¾ oz / 2 ⅓ cups plain flour plus additional for flouring board
1 teaspoon salt
115 g / 4 oz / 1 stick cold, unsalted butter, cut into small pieces
100 ml / 3 ½ fl oz / ⅓ cup+2 tablespoons cold dry white wine

FOR THE FILLING:
2 (112-g / 4-oz) tins tuna, drained
4 tablespoons tomato sauce (page 239) or tinned tomato sauce
1 hard-cooked egg, chopped
1 tablespoon chopped flat-leaf parsley
1 tablespoon brandy
100 g / 3 ½ oz / ⅔ cup drained pimiento-stuffed olives, finely chopped
2 tablespoons finely chopped onion
Salt
Freshly-ground black pepper
1 teaspoon vinegar or lemon juice
Pinch of cayenne

FOR FRYING:
Olive oil

FOR THE DOUGH: Combine the flour and salt in a food processor. Add the butter and pulse until the mixture resembles coarse meal. Add the wine and process 30 seconds until flour begins to clump.

Turn the dough out onto a lightly floured board. Knead very briefly until dough is combined. Cover with plastic wrap and refrigerate for at least 2 hours or up to 24 hours.

FOR THE FILLING: Combine the tuna, tomato sauce, egg, parsley, brandy, olives, onion, salt, pepper, vinegar, and cayenne. Taste the mixture. It should be strongly seasoned. If necessary, add more salt, vinegar, or cayenne.

Divide the ball of dough in half, keeping one half refrigerated. Place the piece of dough on a lightly floured board. Pat it down with the rolling pin until it is slightly softened and flattened enough to start rolling. Roll the dough out as thinly as possible, sprinkling board and rolling pin with flour as needed.

Use a biscuit-cutter to cut circles (85 mm / 3 ½ in). Gather up scraps, press them together and refrigerate. Place a spoonful of the filling on bottom half of each round of dough. Dip a finger in water and moisten the edges of the bottom half. Fold the top half of the circle over the filling and press the edges together. Use the flat, butt-end of a knife to crimp the edges. Place each empanadilla, as filled, onto a tray.

When all of the circles are filled and sealed, roll out the second half of the dough in the same manner. Cut circles, fill, and seal the empanadillas. Then roll out the remaining scraps of dough, cut circles and fill.

FOR FRYING: Heat the oil in a deep pan to a depth of at least 25 mm / 1 in until almost smoking (180ºC / 360ºF). Fry the empanadillas, a few at a time, until they are golden-brown, 5 to 6 minutes. Remove with a skimmer and drain on paper towels. Continue frying the remaining empanadillas.

Serve hot or room temperature.

VARIATION: To bake the turnovers, place them on an ungreased baking sheet. Brush the tops with beaten egg and bake in preheated 195ºC / 375ºF oven until golden, 20 to 25 minutes.

Bienmesabe
CRISPY BITES OF MARINATED FISH

This is a popular tapa throughout Andalusia. *Bienmesabe* means, more or less, "yummies." The tapa is also called *cazón en adobo*. *Cazón* is dogfish, a kind of shark, which is perked up nicely with a tangy, adobo marinade. Any solid-fleshed fish, such as angler (monkfish), could be substituted.

Makes about 45 pieces.

900 g / 2 lb shark or angler fish (monkfish) fillets
3 tablespoons olive oil
5 tablespoons wine vinegar
1 tablespoon water
3 cloves chopped garlic
¼ teaspoon pimentón (paprika)
1 teaspoon crumbled dry oregano
¼ teaspoon freshly ground black pepper
½ teaspoon salt
Flour for dredging fish
Olive oil for frying

Cut the fish into 4-cm / 1 ½-in cubes, discarding any skin and bone. Put the cubes in a non-reactive container.

Mix together the oil, vinegar, water, garlic, pimentón, oregano, pepper and salt. Pour over the fish and mix well. Marinate for at least 6 hours or overnight.

Drain the fish well, dredge it in flour, shake off the excess and fry the pieces, a few at a time, in hot oil until golden and crisp. Drain on paper towels and serve hot.

Calamares Fritos
FRIED SQUID RINGS

Did you think they were fried onion rings the first time this tapa was set down in front of you? Fried squid rings are one of the emblematic tapas in bars from one end of the country to the other. In Spain, they are rarely served with anything more complicated than lemon wedges, although in tapa bars in San Francisco and London, a red pepper garlic mayonnaise (page 250) might accompany them. For how to clean the squid, see page 194. You can use this recipe for preparing any kind of fried fish. A typical "mixed fish fry" would include fresh anchovies, fillets of hake, and a few prawns as well as the squid.

Makes 6 tapas.

4 medium squid, each about 175 g / 6 oz, cleaned
Flour, for dredging
Olive oil, for frying
Salt
Lemon wedges, to serve

Use a sharp knife or kitchen scissors to cut the squid crosswise into rings about 12 mm / ½ in wide. Cut the tentacles in half. Dredge the rings, tentacles and wing flaps in flour, coating them well.

Heat oil in a deep frying pan. Scoop up a handful of floured squid and place in a sieve. Shake the sieve to knock off excess flour.

Fry the squid in hot oil until golden on both sides, about 2 minutes. Remove and drain on paper towels. Fry remaining squid in the same manner.

Place the fried squid on a serving dish, sprinkle with salt and serve hot, accompanied by lemon wedges.

Tigres
"TIGERS" (STUFFED MUSSELS)

These "tigers" are from Madrid--chopped mussels with a rich béchamel sauce, fried in their shells until the tops are golden. But, who knows why they are called "tigers" in tapa bars? In Santiago de Compostela in Galicia, *tigres rabiosos* are also mussels, but those "tigers" are cooked in a spicy tomato sauce.

Makes 14 to18 pieces.

1 kg / 2 ¼ lb mussels (about 2 dozen), scrubbed
    and beards removed
2 tablespoons olive oil
1 tablespoon finely chopped onion
2 tablespoons plain flour

4 tablespoons white wine
120 ml / 4 fl oz / ½ cup mussel liquid
1 egg beaten with 1 tablespoon water
5 tablespoons fine dry bread crumbs
120 ml / 4 fl oz / ½ cup olive oil for frying

Put the cleaned mussels in a deep pan with 140 ml / ¼ pint / ⅔ cup of water. Cover the pan and shake over high heat until mussels open. Remove from heat and discard any mussels that do not open.

When mussels are cool enough to handle, remove the mussel meat from the shells, saving18 of the shells. Chop the mussels; strain and reserve the mussel liquid.

Heat the oil in a saucepan and sauté the onion until it is softened, without letting it brown. Stir in the flour, cook for a minute, stirring, then whisk in the wine and the mussel liquid. Cook, stirring, until the mixture is thickened and smooth. Stir in the chopped mussels.

Put a spoonful of this white sauce onto each mussel shell and smooth it level with the top of the shell. Refrigerate until the sauce is firmly set, at least 1 hour.

Place the beaten egg and the bread crumbs in two shallow bowls. Dip the mussels, open face down, first into egg, then bread crumbs. Arrange them on a tray in a single layer. (The mussels can be prepared up to this point, then frozen. Freeze them in one layer, then pack them carefully in a freezer bag or plastic container. Let them thaw one hour before continuing with the preparation.) Otherwise, fry them immediately before serving.

To fry the mussels, heat enough oil to cover the bottom of a frying pan. Fry them in two or three batches, breaded side down, until golden brown. Add additional oil between batches as needed. Drain briefly on paper towels and serve hot.

Gambas en Gabardinas
PRAWNS IN MACKINTOSH (BATTER-FRIED)

On your Madrid tapas crawl, you will surely encounter this favourite—prawns fried in a puffy batter. Supposedly, the batter-dipped and fried prawns look like they're wearing coats or mackintoshes. These are good served with a spicy tomato sauce (page 226) or piquillo pepper sauce (page 251). Oysters or scallops also can be fried with this fritter batter.

Makes about 10 tapas (allowing 3 prawns per person).

450 g / 1 lb raw king prawns (jumbo shrimp)
1 egg, beaten
1 tablespoon olive oil
4 tablespoons water
½ teaspoon salt
¼ teaspoon bicarbonate of soda (baking soda)
100 g / 3 ½ oz / ¾ cup+1 tablespoon plain flour
Olive oil for frying

Peel the prawns, leaving the tails intact. Refrigerate.

Combine the egg, oil, water, salt, bicarbonate and flour to make a batter that is thick enough to coat the prawns. If necessary, thin with water, a few drops at a time. Let the batter rest 1 hour.

Heat the oil to 180ºC / 350ºF. Dip the prawns by their tails into the batter and fry in the hot oil. The batter should puff slightly. Remove the prawns when golden.

Pavías de Merluza
BATTER-FRIED FISH FINGERS

Here's a popular tapa from the Triana *barrio*, district, in Sevilla, where it's usually made with bacalao, salt cod. This version, with fresh cod or hake, is just as acceptable, and a whole lot easier (no soaking of the salt cod).

Makes 10 tapas or 4 to 6 main dishes.

½ teaspoon active dry yeast
Pinch of saffron, crushed
Hand-hot water
100 g / 3 ½ oz / ¾ cup+1 tablespoon plain flour
½ teaspoon salt
1 tablespoon olive oil
1 tablespoon finely chopped parsley

1 clove garlic, finely chopped
1 kg / 1 lb 3 oz fresh or frozen hake or cod fillets
Salt
Olive oil for frying
Strips of tinned red pimiento or piquillo pepper sauce (page 251)

Place the yeast and the saffron in two small bowls. Add 2 tablespoons hot water to the yeast and 2 tablespoons hot water to the saffron. Allow the yeast to bubble for 5 minutes.

Place the flour in a bowl and combine with the salt. Make a well in the centre of the flour and stir in the oil, yeast and saffron. Stir in enough additional hot water, about 8 tablespoons, to make a smooth batter about the consistency of thick cream.

Allow the batter to stand for 1 hour or, covered and refrigerated, for up to 24 hours. Bring to room temperature before proceeding with the recipe. Stir in the parsley and garlic.

Cut the fish fillets into strips about 7 cm x 2 cm / 2 ¾ in x ¾ in. If using fresh fish, salt it lightly and allow to stand 30 minutes. Do not salt frozen fish. Pat the fish dry.

Place oil in a deep frying pan to a depth of 5 cm / 2 in. Heat to 180ºC / 355ºF.

Dredge the fish fingers in the batter. Fry them in hot oil until golden on all sides, 2 to 3 minutes. Remove with a skimmer and drain on paper towels. Serve the fish fingers hot with a strip of red pimiento or piquillo pepper sauce.

Rollitos de Berenjena y Langostinos
AUBERGINE AND PRAWN ROLLUPS

Crisp on the outside, the aubergine makes a creamy layer encasing the prawn. Don't let the oil get too hot—you want to let the prawn and aubergine cook through in the time it takes to brown the outside of the rolls.

These rolls are good served with a dipping sauce, such as piquillo pepper sauce (page 251) or garlic mayonnaise with saffron (page 250).

Makes 12 tapas or 4 starters.

1 medium aubergine (eggplant), about 340 g / 12 oz
Salt
12 king prawns (jumbo shrimp), peeled
1 egg, beaten with 1 teaspoon water
115 g / 4 oz / 1 cup fine, dry bread crumbs
Oil for frying (about 240 ml / 8 fl oz / 1 cup)

Cut off and discard the aubergine stem. Slice the aubergine lengthwise very thinly (4 mm / ⅛ in), discarding 2 outer slices with skin. You should have 12 slices. Place the slices in a colander and sprinkle liberally with salt. Allow to stand for 45 minutes.

Pat the aubergine dry with paper towels. Place a prawn across the wide end of a slice and roll up the aubergine around the prawn. Fasten the roll with a wooden toothpick.

When all the slices are rolled, dip them, one by one, into beaten egg, then roll in bread crumbs. Place on a tray in a single layer. (The rolls can be prepared up to 4 hours in advance and kept, refrigerated.)

Add oil to a frying pan to a depth of at least 6 mm / ¼ in. Heat the oil on medium heat until it is shimmering, but not smoking. Fry the rolls, a few at a time, until they are browned on all sides, about 4 minutes total. Remove and drain on paper towels. Serve immediately.

Tortillitas de Camarones
SHRIMP FRITTERS

In Cádiz, these fritters are made with teensy, live shrimp, which are folded into a pancake batter. You can adapt the recipe, using chopped prawns.

Makes 18 (7 ½-cm / 3-in) fritters.

110 g / 4 oz / 1 cup plain flour
3 tablespoons finely chopped spring onion with some of green
1 tablespoon chopped parsley
½ teaspoon salt
Pinch of cayenne
1 teaspoon olive oil
240 ml / 8 fl oz / 1 cup water
170 g / 6 oz / 1 cup raw, peeled, chopped prawns (shrimp)
Olive oil for frying

In a bowl combine the flour, onion, parsley, salt, cayenne, oil and water. Stir to blend thoroughly and refrigerate the batter for at least one hour.

Fold in the chopped prawns and enough additional water to make a loose pancake batter.

Heat a frying pan with enough oil to cover the bottom. Drop the batter by spoonfuls into the pan. Flatten it with a spatula. Fry until browned on the bottom, then turn and brown the reverse side. The fritters should be thin and crisp. Continue frying the fritters, adding oil as needed. Drain on paper towels. Serve immediately.

Tortillitas de Bacalao con Miel de Caña
COD FRITTERS WITH MOLASSES

This tapa is typical in Málaga, where sugar refineries, established at the end of the 1500s, produced cane syrup, a sort of light molasses, which entered the local culinary tradition.

You could use molasses, bee's honey or golden syrup in this recipe. In fact, you need very little. It is the intriguing contrast of salty and sweet that makes this an outstanding dish.

Makes about 12 fritters.

115 g / 4 oz dry salt cod, soaked for 24 hours in several changes of water
1 tablespoon parsley, chopped
1 clove garlic, finely chopped
Pinch of crushed saffron
1 egg, separated
100 g / 3 ½ oz / ¾ cup+1tablespoon plain flour
1 teaspoon baking powder
Olive oil for frying
2 tablespoons molasses or honey

Drain the salt cod and put in a pan with water to cover and bring just to a simmer, then remove from heat. Drain and save the liquid. When the cod is cool enough to handle, remove any bones and skin and flake the fish.

Combine the parsley, garlic, saffron and egg yolk. Beat in 240 ml / 8 fl oz / 1 cup of the reserved liquid. Combine the flour and baking powder. Stir in the liquid ingredients. Add the flaked cod. The batter should be the consistency of pancake batter. Let it rest for an hour.

Beat the egg white until stiff and fold into the batter.

Add oil to a frying pan to a depth of 25 mm / 1 in and heat until shimmering. Drop batter by tablespoons, turning to brown on both sides. Drain the fritters on paper towels. Serve them hot, drizzled with molasses or honey.

Tortillitas de Espinacas
SPINACH FRITTERS

These fritters are like diminutive pancakes. You could serve them for brunch with sliced cheese.

Makes 20 small fritters.

400 g / 14 oz fresh spinach or chard leaves
2 tablespoons olive oil
2 cloves garlic, chopped
2 eggs, separated
125 g / 4 ¼ oz / 1 cup+2tablespoons plain flour
½ teaspoon baking powder

2 tablespoons water
Pinch of ground cumin
1 teaspoon salt
Freshly ground black pepper
1 teaspoon wine vinegar
Olive oil for frying

Wash spinach and chop it coarsely. Heat the oil in a frying pan and sauté the spinach and garlic until spinach is wilted.

In a food processor or blender, combine the egg yolks, flour, baking powder and water with the spinach and process until combined. Season with cumin, salt and pepper.

In a clean bowl, beat the egg whites until stiff and add the vinegar. Fold the egg whites into the spinach mixture.

Heat enough oil to coat the surface of the frying pan. Over medium heat, drop spoonfuls of the spinach mixture into the oil. Fry slowly until set and lightly browned on the bottom. Turn the fritters and fry slowly on the reverse side. Add a little more oil to the pan and continue frying the remaining batter. Serve immediately.

Alas de Pollo Empanadas
FRIED CHICKEN WINGS

Crunchy, fried chicken wings with spicy dipping sauce make great tapas. They are a bit messy for finger food, so provide paper napkins. These are best made with the "drumette," the thick joint of the wing. Serve the wings with a dipping sauce, such as Cabrales blue cheese sauce (page 240), caper mayonnaise (page 250) or green chilli sauce with coriander (page 256).

Makes 12 tapas.

12 wing joints (about 680 g / 1 ½ lb)
Salt and pepper
½ teaspoon pimentón (paprika)
Pinch of thyme
2 tablespoons lemon juice

1 egg, beaten
100 g / 3 ½ oz / 1 cup fine dry bread crumbs
Olive oil for frying
Dipping sauce, to serve

Sprinkle the wings with salt, pepper, pimentón, thyme and lemon juice. Let them stand at room temperature for 30 minutes.

Place the egg and crumbs in two shallow bowls. Dip the wings first in egg then roll them in crumbs to coat. Place in a single layer on a tin to dry for 20 minutes.

Heat the oil in a large frying pan. Fry the wings in two batches, turning once, until they are well-browned and cooked through, about 8 minutes. Drain on paper towels. Serve hot or room temperature, accompanied by a dipping sauce. Wings can be fried in advance and reheated in a medium-hot oven for 5 minutes.

Flamenquines de Cerdo
CRISP FRIED PORK ROLLS

This tapa is a speciality of Córdoba and Jaén, where olive oil rules the roost. The crisp fried pork rolls go great with cold draught beer.

Makes 8 rolls.

8 slices boneless pork loin (about 600 g / 1 lb 5 oz)
Salt and pepper
8 thin slices serrano ham (120 g / 4 oz)
60 g / 2 oz cheese (such as Manchego), cut in strips
Flour for dredging
½ teaspoon salt

⅛ teaspoon freshly ground black pepper
Pinch of thyme
¼ teaspoon pimentón (paprika)
1 egg, beaten with 1 tablespoon water
60 g / 2 oz / ½ cup fine dry bread crumbs
Olive oil for frying
Lemon wedges, to serve

Place the slices of loin between layers of plastic wrap and pound them to a thickness of 6 mm / ¼ in. Sprinkle them with salt and pepper. Lay a slice of ham on top of each slice and place strips of cheese crosswise on top. Roll up the slices, Swiss-roll style (jelly-roll style), and secure them with wooden toothpicks.

Combine the flour, salt, pepper, thyme and pimentón in a dish. Place the beaten egg and bread crumbs in two shallow bowls.

First dredge the rolls in the flour mixture, patting off excess. Then put them in the beaten egg and rock the dish back and forth to coat the rolls with egg. Remove them and roll in the bread crumbs, taking special care to seal the ends with egg and crumbs. Let the rolls dry for at least 30 minutes. (They can be prepared in advance and refrigerated, but bring them to room temperature before cooking.)

Heat oil in a frying pan to a depth of 25 mm / 1 in. Fry the rolls on high heat for 3 minutes, then lower heat to medium and fry until they are very browned and crisp on all sides, about 5 minutes. The meat should be cooked through and the cheese melted. Drain briefly on paper towels and serve hot with lemon wedges.

Emparedados de Jamón y Queso
FRIED HAM AND CHEESE SANDWICHES

These are a dream version of a cheese toasty. Use Manchego or smoked Idiazábal cheese for superb flavour.

Makes 16 tapas.

150 g / 5 ¼ oz thinly sliced serrano ham
150 g / 5 ¼ oz sliced Idiazábal cheese
8 slices sandwich bread
100 ml / 3 ½ fl oz / ⅓ cup milk
1 egg, beaten
40 g / 1 ½ oz / ⅓ cup fine dry breadcrumbs
Olive oil for frying

Layer the ham and cheese on four of the bread slices. Top each with a slice of bread and press them together. Trim off the crusts and cut the sandwiches diagonally into quarters.

Dip each piece into milk, then beaten egg, then breadcrumbs. Heat enough oil in a frying pan to cover the bottom and fry the sandwiches, a few at a time, until browned on both sides. Serve hot.

Patatas Bravas
FRIED POTATOES WITH HOT SAUCE

Invented at Café Bravas in Madrid, this tapa has taken the country by storm. Each bar reinvents the sauce. What you need to know: the potatoes are cut in cubes and the sauce should be quite spicy.

Makes 6 to 8 tapas.

120 ml / 4 fl oz / ½ cup tinned tomato sauce
1 clove garlic, crushed
1 tablespoon olive oil
¼ teaspoon ground cumin
1 teaspoon hot pimentón (spicy paprika) or pinch of cayenne
½ teaspoon oregano, crumbled
1 tablespoon wine vinegar
6 tablespoons water
900 g / 2 lb mature baking potatoes
Olive oil for frying
Salt
Garlic mayonnaise (page 248), optional

Combine the tomato sauce, garlic, oil, cumin, pimentón, oregano, vinegar and water in a small saucepan. Bring to a boil and simmer 5 minutes. Reserve the sauce.

Peel the potatoes and cut them into 4-cm / 1 ½-in cubes.

Place oil in a deep frying pan to a depth of 25 mm / 1 in. Heat the oil until it is shimmering, but not smoking, 180ºC / 360ºF. Fry the potato cubes for 2 minutes. Reduce heat so the oil is just bubbling. Fry the potatoes for 10 minutes or until they are cooked all the way through. Then raise the heat again and fry until they are golden and crisp, about 3 minutes more.

Drain the potatoes on paper towels. Sprinkle with salt. Heap them in a bowl. Dribble the sauce over them. If desired, serve garlic mayonnaise with the potatoes as well.

Pencas de Acelgas Rellenas
STUFFED CHARD STEMS

Chard is a versatile vegetable because the stems can be cooked in one way and the green, leafy tops, which resemble spinach, in another. Choose chard with wide stalks to prepare this recipe. If desired, thinly sliced ham can be sandwiched in the filling with the cheese.

Makes 6 tapas.

12 chard stems, 11 cm / 4 ½ inches long and at least 5 cm / 2 in wide
60 g / 2 oz / ½ cup grated cheese
70 g / 2 ½ oz / ½ cup+1 tablespoon plain flour
1 egg, well beaten
Olive oil for frying

Trim the chard stems of strings. Cook the stems in boiling salted water until tender, about 8 minutes. Drain.

Place 6 pieces on work surface. Spread each with a spoonful of grated cheese. Top each with another piece of chard and squeeze the edges together slightly, sandwiching in the cheese.

Place the flour and beaten egg in two shallow bowls. Dip the pieces of chard first in flour, then egg, then again in flour.

Heat sufficient oil to cover the bottom of a frying pan. Fry the floured pieces of chard until browned on both sides.

Drain briefly on paper towels. If desired, cut the pieces in half. Serve hot.

Pimientos de Padrón
FRIED PADRÓN PEPPERS

At the bars in the Zona Vieja of Santiago de Compostela, these fried green peppers are a favourite tapa. Padrón is a town not far from Santiago where the peppers are grown. Picked when still tiny (35 to 40 mm / 1 ½ to 1 ¾ in), the peppers are famed for their bittersweet flavour and the Russian-roulette chance that about one in ten is a fiery-hot chilli. If Padrón peppers are not available, use whole, skinny, thin-skinned frying peppers or green bell peppers, stem and seeds discarded and flesh cut into strips.

Take care not to let the oil get too hot—the peppers should not brown. The peppers make a great side dish with steak, chops or fried eggs. To eat them, use the stems as handles to pick them up. You eat the tiny seeds too, then discard the stem.

Makes 6 tapas or side dishes.

400 g / 14 oz Padrón peppers (about 75 peppers)
Olive oil for frying
Coarse salt, to serve

Wash the peppers and dry them thoroughly. Place oil in a large frying pan to a depth of 18 mm / ¾ in. Place on medium heat. Fry the peppers in two batches, carefully turning them in the oil, until they are wrinkled and soft, but not browned, about 5 minutes. Skim the peppers out and drain on paper towels. Sprinkle with salt. Serve hot or room temperature.

Pez de Tierra
"LAND FISH" (FRIED AUBERGINE)

Aubergine (eggplant) prepared this way is sometimes called *pez de tierra*, "land fish", because it resembles fried fish-fingers. Serve it accompanied by *salmorejo*, gazpacho cream sauce (page 252) or red pepper mayonnaise (page 250). Fried aubergine is also delicious with a drizzle of molasses. It may sound odd, but a trickle of sweet sets off the salty, fried aubergine very nicely.

Makes 8 tapas or 4 starters.

1 medium aubergine (eggplant), about 340 g / 12 oz
45 g / 1 ½ oz / ⅓ cup+1 tablespoon plain flour
¼ teaspoon ground cumin
⅛ teaspoon ground black pepper
Olive oil for frying
Salt

Peel the aubergine and cut it as for chips (fries), in strips about 9 cm / 3 ½ in long by 18 mm / ¾ in wide. Combine the flour, cumin and pepper in a bowl. Add the aubergine strips and toss to coat them with flour.

Heat the oil in a deep frying pan. Fry the aubergine pieces in two batches until golden-brown, about 2 minutes. Remove, drain on paper towels and sprinkle with salt. Serve hot.

Boquerones del Campo
Langostinos de la Huerta

"FIELD ANCHOVIES" (GREEN BEANS)
"GARDEN CRAYFISH" (ASPARAGUS)

Vegetables with a giggle—they are masquerading as fish. Runner beans, crisply fried, really do resemble fresh, fried anchovies! Enjoy these right out of the frying pan. They don't really need any sauce—just a squeeze of lemon. Should you have leftovers, cut them up and combine them with a tomato sauce and toss with cooked pasta.

You can use this fritter batter for other vegetables as well—cooked cauliflower florets, mushrooms, courgettes (zucchini), artichoke hearts—or pieces of fish, shellfish or sausage. For *calamares de campo*, "field squid," dip rings of green pepper and onions into the batter and fry them.

Makes 10 tapas or starters.

2 eggs
1 tablespoon olive oil
2 tablespoons finely chopped parsley
1 clove garlic, finely chopped
½ teaspoon salt
120 ml / 4 fl oz / ½ cup water
120 g / 4 ¼ oz / 1 cup+1tablespoon plain flour plus additional for dredging
1 teaspoon baking powder
460 g / 1 lb runner beans (flat romano beans)
460 g / 1 lb fresh asparagus spears
Olive oil for frying
Lemon wedges, to serve

Beat the eggs together in a bowl with 1 tablespoon of oil. Stir in the parsley, garlic, salt and water. Combine the flour and baking powder in another bowl. Stir the egg mixture into the flour until smooth. Allow the batter to stand for 1 hour at room temperature or, covered and refrigerated, up to 8 hours.

Top and tail the runner beans. Cook them in boiling, salted water until crisp-tender, about 4 minutes from the time the water returns to the boil. Drain and rinse in cold water to stop the cooking. Drain well.

Break off butt ends of asparagus. Cook the spears in boiling, salted water until they are crisp-tender, about 5 minutes from the time the water returns to the boil. Drain and rinse in cold water to stop the cooking. Drain well.

Place flour and batter in two shallow bowls. Dredge the cooked beans and cooked asparagus first in flour, then in the batter.

Heat oil in a deep frying pan to 180ºC / 360ºF. Fry the beans, then asparagus, a few pieces at a time until lightly browned, about 2 minutes. Remove with a skimmer to paper towels to drain. Serve beans and asparagus immediately, accompanied by lemon.

ASPARAGUS, WILD OR TAME

Asparagus, wild or cultivated, fresh or tinned, green or white, is a superb ingredient for creating tapas. Folded into eggs with bits of ham, it fills out a tortilla. Served cold, with a sassy vinaigrette (page 254), it makes a lovely starter.

Skinny stalks of wild asparagus, *esparragos trigueros*, come into markets in earliest spring. Wild asparagus is slightly bitter and is best chopped and blanched in boiling water for 2 minutes. Afterwards, it can be sautéed with ham and scrambled with eggs for a typical tapa, *revuelto*.

To cook fresh cultivated asparagus: Snap off the butt ends of the stalks. Bring salted water to the boil in a frying pan. Place the asparagus flat, in a single layer, in the water and cook, uncovered, six to seven minutes. To check on whether it's done, lift a spear on a fork. If it bends slightly, but doesn't droop off the fork, it's ready. Drain it and refresh in cold water to stop the cooking. Asparagus to be cooked on the griddle (or on a barbecue) should be first peeled. Use a vegetable peeler to shave away the thin outer skin.

Salsas y Aliños

SAUCES, DRESSINGS, DIPS & SPREADS

Salsas y Aliños
SAUCES, DRESSINGS, DIPS & SPREADS

Olive Oil—The Main Ingredient

Tomato Sauce (*Salsa de Tomate Frito*)

Cabrales Blue Cheese Sauce (*Salsa Cabrales*)

Quince Sauce (*Salsa de Membrillo*)

Catalan Red Pepper Sauce (*Romesco*)

Fig and Sweet Wine Sauce (*Salsa de Higos y Vino Dulce*)

Olive Sauce with Sherry (*Salsa de Aceitunas*)

Black Olive Spread (*Olivada*)

Olive Pâté (*Paté de Aceitunas*)

Garlic Mayonnaise I (*Alioli I*)

Garlic Mayonnaise II (*Alioli II*)

Piquillo Red Pepper Sauce (*Salsa de Pimientos Piquillos*)

Gazpacho Cream (*Salmorejo*)

Vinaigrette (*Salsa Vinagreta*)

Sauce for Griddled Foods (*Aliño*)

Green Chilli Sauce with Coriander (*Mojo Verde*)

Red Chilli Sauce (*Mojo Colorado*)

Many tapas start out simple—meat or shellfish on a griddle; plain, boiled vegetables; tuna from a tin—but get a dash of pizzazz—the *olé* factor—with the addition of a savoury, flavour-packed sauce. A dab of pungent garlic mayonnaise; a dribble of *romesco*, made with pounded peppers and almonds, or a splash of tangy vinaigrette can turn the mundane into the sublime.

What, exactly, is a sauce, anyway? The recipes in this chapter are for sauces that make flavourful additions to foods, separate preparations to be served under, over or beside a food. But, in Spanish cooking, sauces are frequently the cooking medium—liquid and seasonings added to food while it cooks. Examples of these are salt cod in garlic pil pil sauce; kidneys in Sherry sauce; meatballs with almond sauce, and shellfish balls in green sauce. (Please see the Index to find the recipes for these and other cook-in sauces.)

In Spain sauce is synonymous with olive oil. The most basic sauces are just combinations of flavourful olive oil with, perhaps, garlic, salt, a few herbs—hardly more than what you would call a "salad dressing". The most complex of Spanish sauces also have olive oil as their star ingredient. Even in Galicia and Asturias, regions that produce excellent butter, olive oil is used in typical sauces.

Many traditional sauces were once confected with a mortar and pestle, which was used to crush nuts, garlic and herbs and to emulsify. Nowadays, of course, you can zip through these sauces in an electric blender or food processor in minutes.

Few Spanish sauces are flour-thickened, although sometimes bread, finely ground nuts or biscuit (cookie) crumbs serve as thickeners. Many cold sauces—mayonnaise is the best example—are thickened by an olive oil emulsion.

Besides olive oil, other ingredients in Spanish sauces are—but of course—garlic, almonds, hazelnuts, sweet red pepper, pimentón (paprika), saffron, and, oh, yes, tomatoes.

Adobo and *escabeche* are marinade sauces that were used to preserve fish or meat before the days of refrigeration. They are still enjoyed because they add so much flavour. Adobo is a marinade for raw foods. The primary ingredients are olive oil, vinegar, garlic, oregano and paprika. Escabeche, a favourite with fish and with partridge, is similar, but might contain bay leaf, thyme, carrots and onion, peppercorns, even chilli pepper. Usually cooked foods are put into the escabeche marinade, which serves as a dressing in serving.

Aliño is an uncooked sauce, similar to vinaigrette or salad dressing, that is drizzled on cooked foods such as griddled fish or boiled vegetables.

Herbs are used discreetly in Spanish sauces—a sprig of thyme in a rabbit dish; bay leaf in meat stews; oregano in vinegar marinades; wild fennel with fish. The exception is parsley, which is used lavishly in many different dishes, raw and cooked. In the Basque country, *salsa verde*, green sauce, made with olive oil, garlic and a whole handful of chopped, flat-leaf parsley, goes with many seafood dishes.

Although the Spanish word for sauce is *salsa*, take note, that salsa in Spain is never the chilli-hot dipping sauce used with Mexican and Tex-Mex foods.

◢ OLIVE OIL—THE MAIN INGREDIENT

If you're starting out to prepare tapas at home, the first item on your shopping list should be extra virgin olive oil. You're going to need it for almost every recipe in this book!

Olive oil has been part of Spanish cooking since Greek and Phoenician times. After Spain became part of the Roman Empire, the Romans really exploited Spanish oil, shipping it back to Rome in huge amphorae. When the Moors took over in 711, they extended the cultivation of olive trees even further.

Today, Spain produces more olive oil than any other country in the world—between 35 to 47 percent of the world-wide production. There are 309 million olive trees extending over 5 million acres of Spain's landscape. About 75 percent of Spanish olive oil comes from Andalusia, southern Spain. The province of Jaén alone produces more olive oil than all of Greece. You get the picture? Olive oil is the main ingredient in Spanish cooking.

Olives for oil are picked when they are ripe. Most varieties—there are dozens in Spain—do not turn really black when ripe, but a greenish-purplish colour. The harvest begins in late November and continues until around the first of February.

The pickers spread nets or tarps under the trees to catch the olives. Then they use long poles to thrash the branches, causing the fruit to drop.

The olives are collected in baskets and hauled to the oil mill. The sooner they are pressed, the better will be the oil.

In modern mills, a centrifugal process is used to extract the oil. After crushing, the olives are mixed with warmed water, then spun at high speed to separate the oil from the water. The resulting product is virgin olive oil. Its colour can vary from pale gold to amber to almost green, depending on the variety of olive.

How good that oil tastes depends on several factors, such as the variety of olive, the soil, the climate, the ripeness of the olives, but, most importantly, how the olives were picked, transported, stored and milled.

Virgin olive oil is oil that has been extracted solely by mechanical means—crushing and pressing, without the use of

high temperatures or chemicals that alter the oil's composition.

But, what's with the label of "extra virgin olive oil"? How can a virgin be "extra"? It has to do with how much man-handling was involved in the production! Careful picking, transporting, storage and milling produces the finest extra virgin oil. It is the most expensive olive oil, though even amongst the extra virgins there are variations in quality and price. For example, those made by artisan methods might be better in flavour and much more expensive than a supermarket brand produced by a big cooperative. Organic olive oil also is pricier, as are those oils that have "designer labels", *denominación de origen*, DO, designated origin.

Once you begin sampling from the range of virgin oils, you will begin to appreciate differences in olive varietals, too (sort of like distinguishing between Cabernet-Sauvignon and Merlot). Arbequina olive oil is extraordinarily delicate, best used raw. (Dribble it over grilled fish, for instance.) Picual oil has a peppery bite and is remarkably stable at high temperatures. It's a good choice for sautéing and for frying. Hojiblanca lends a rich fruitiness to sauces and is perfect in gazpacho.

As for the non-virgins—they are simply labelled "olive oil," or *aceite de oliva*. This, in fact, is refined olive oil. It comes from virgin oil that, after extraction, is deemed to be too strong or with off flavours or too high in oleic acid to be consumed virgin. It is refined—as other seed oils are refined, by a process of neutralization, decolouration and deodorization. A distillation process is involved, which changes the structure of the oil. Once purified, it is then mixed with a small portion of good virgin oil in order to restore some of the olive flavour. These oils are the least expensive. Because they're cheap, they are useful for deep frying or when you are using large quantities of oil. But, for flavour and cooking properties, choose extra virgin oil.

Virgin olive oil has natural protection against oxidation and rancidity. However, don't keep it longer than 12 to18 months. Don't refrigerate olive oil, but do keep it in a moderately cool place, tightly capped and, most importantly, protected from the light. A dark cupboard is fine. Although some oils are marketed in plastic containers, extra virgin oils are best preserved in glass.

Serve olive oil on breakfast toast with marmalade. Use it in cake baking. In stir-fries and sautés. Olive oil makes the best chips (fries) in the world. Fry eggs in it. Drizzle it on baked potatoes. Toss it with cooked vegetables. On popcorn. Sprinkled on sliced fresh tomatoes. Use it for browning meat. In marinades. Baste the Christmas turkey with it. Make sauce to serve with tapas.

Salsa de Tomate Frito
TOMATO SAUCE

This is the "mother of all sauces" in Spanish cuisine. Use it as an accompaniment to cooked foods or as a cooking sauce. Its substitute is tinned, prepared tomato sauce (not paste or concentrate).

Makes 350 ml / 12 ½ fl oz / 1 ½ cups.

1 large tin (780-800 g / 27-28 oz) plum tomatoes, drained, liquid reserved
2 tablespoons olive oil
1 medium onion, chopped
2 cloves chopped garlic
4 tablespoons chopped flat-leaf parsley
1 teaspoon pimentón (paprika)
Pinch of ground cumin
1 bay leaf
Salt and pepper
Pinch of sugar
4 tablespoons white wine or reserved tomato liquid

Cut out stem ends of tomatoes and break the tomatoes up slightly. Heat oil in a saucepan and sauté the onion and garlic until onion begins to turn golden, 5 minutes. Add the parsley and pimentón. Stir over medium heat 30 seconds. Add the tomatoes, cumin, bay leaf, salt, pepper and sugar. Add wine or tomato liquid.

Bring to the boil, cover, and simmer until tomatoes are thickened, 25 to 35 minutes. Discard the bay leaf.

Purée the sauce in a blender. If desired, sieve the sauce to make it even smoother. Serve the sauce hot or room temperature.

Salsa Cabrales
CABRALES BLUE CHEESE SAUCE

Cabrales is a distinctive blue cheese from Asturias—sharp, but remarkably creamy in consistency. It makes a delightful dressing or dip when thinned with wine or, in the Asturian style, dry cider. Serve this sauce with chicory leaves (Belgian endive) for dipping; with charcoal-grilled entrecote steaks or spooned over a salad of frisée, sliced pears and toasted almonds.

Makes 200 ml / 7 fl oz / ⅔ cup.

150 g / 5 oz Cabrales (Asturian) blue cheese
2 tablespoons chopped onions
75 ml / 2 ½ fl oz / ¼ cup white wine, cider or cava (sparkling wine)
Pinch of cumin seed

Place the cheese in a blender with onions, wine and cumin seed. Blend until smooth. Serve immediately or keep, covered and refrigerated, up to 3 days.

Salsa de Membrillo
QUINCE SAUCE

Quince is a fruit so rich in pectin that, when cooked with sugar, it sets up into a solid paste that can be cut into cubes *(dulce de membrillo)*. A handy ingredient to keep in the pantry, quince paste can be turned into a quick sauce, delicious served with pork, with cheese croquettes, with foie gras, with duck. The sauce thickens as it cools. Serve it room temperature or reheat it in a small pan.

Makes 210 ml / 7 fl oz.

125 g / 4 ½ oz quince paste
1 tablespoon Sherry vinegar
120 ml / 4 fl oz / ½ cup boiling water

Cut the quince paste into pieces and place in
a blender with the vinegar and boiling water.
Blend until quince is smooth.

Romesco
CATALAN RED PEPPER SAUCE

This is the most emblematic sauce of Spanish-Catalan cuisine. It's traditionally made with dry sweet peppers, crushed in a mortar with almonds and hazelnuts, sometimes with roasted tomato as well, all emulsified with extra virgin olive oil. In this recipe, pimentón (paprika) substitutes for the crushed dry peppers. Serve romesco with boiled vegetables, griddled shellfish, poached fish or charcoal-grilled spring onions. It's an all-purpose sauce that can accompany hot or cold foods. If you are serving it with seafood, use fish stock to thin the sauce. Otherwise, add just enough water to make a sauce the consistency of pouring cream.

Makes 300 ml / ½ pint / 1 ¼ cups.

2 tablespoons pimentón (paprika)
4 tablespoons red wine
150 ml / ¼ pint / ⅔ cup extra virgin olive oil
12 skinned almonds
12 skinned hazelnuts
1 slice bread, crusts removed
3 cloves garlic
Pinch of dried mint
1 tablespoon wine vinegar
Pinch crushed red chilli flakes
Salt
Water or fish stock (about 120 ml / 4 fl oz / ½ cup)

Stir the pimentón and red wine together to make a paste.

In a small frying pan, heat 2 tablespoons of the oil and fry the almonds, hazelnuts, bread and garlic until bread is toasted. Remove and transfer them to a blender or food processor with the pimentón paste, mint, vinegar, chilli and salt. Blend to a smooth paste. Gradually blend in the remaining oil. Add enough water to thin the sauce to the consistency of thick cream.

Salsa de Higos y Vino Dulce
FIG AND SWEET WINE SAUCE

Serve this sauce with foie gras, duck breast, pork fillet (tenderloin) or with any dish where the sweetness of the fruit makes a good contrast. Pedro Ximénez wine is a superb choice, but Muscatel or oloroso Sherry could be used instead. If desired, add a splash of Sherry vinegar to the sauce for a sweet and sour effect.

Makes 250 ml / 8 fl oz.

150 g / 5 ½ oz dry figs
1 tablespoon olive oil
3 shallots, chopped
Strip of orange zest, finely chopped
120 ml / 4 fl oz / ½ cup Pedro Ximénez wine
140 ml / ¼ pint / ⅔ cup water or chicken stock
Salt and pepper
Pinch of ground cloves

Cut out the stems and rinse the figs in running water. Chop them coarsely.

Heat the oil in a small frying pan and sauté the shallots for 3 minutes. Add the orange zest, figs, wine, water, salt, pepper and cloves. Bring to a boil, then cover and simmer until figs are softened, 15 minutes. Serve the sauce hot or room temperature.

Salsa de Aceitunas
OLIVE SAUCE WITH SHERRY

Olives and lemon peel give zest to this sauce, which goes well with grilled fish, duck breast and chicken. Use any variety of pitted olive, green or black, for this recipe. This is a cooked sauce. Two quick olive sauces made in the blender follow.

Makes 250 ml / 8 fl oz / 1 cup.

1 tablespoon olive oil
¼ onion, finely chopped
1 small carrot, finely chopped
1 clove garlic, chopped
1 strip lemon zest, chopped
1 medium tomato, peeled and chopped
100 ml / 3 ½ fl oz / ⅓ cup dry Sherry
½ teaspoon corn flour (cornstarch)
120 ml / 4 fl oz / ½ cup water or chicken stock
Pinch of cumin seed
Pinch of thyme
Pepper
¼ teaspoon salt
80 g / 3 oz / ⅔ cup pitted olives, coarsely chopped

Heat the oil in a medium frying pan and sauté the onion, carrot and garlic until softened, 3 minutes. Add the lemon zest and tomato and cook another 3 minutes.

Add the Sherry. Stir the corn flour into the water or chicken stock and add it to the pan with the cumin, thyme, pepper and salt. Cook, stirring, 2 minutes. Cover and simmer until vegetables are very tender, 25 minutes.

Add the olives and simmer 5 minutes. Serve the sauce hot or room temperature.

Olivada
BLACK OLIVE SPREAD

Serve this olive purée as a dip, sandwich spread or sauce to accompany roast lamb, fried fish or sliced tomatoes.

Makes 200 ml / 7 fl oz / ¾ cup.

125 g / 4 ¼ oz / 1 cup drained and pitted black olives
1 clove garlic, chopped
1 shallot, chopped
1 tablespoon chopped parsley
1 tablespoon lemon juice
2 tablespoons dry Sherry
2 tablespoons extra virgin olive oil
Salt and pepper

Combine all the ingredients in a blender or food processor. Blend until smoothly puréed. Serve cold or room temperature.

Paté de Aceitunas
OLIVE PÂTÉ

This Catalan olive pâté can be served as a topping for toast, a sandwich spread, a sauce for grilled fish or a dressing for boiled potatoes. If possible, use Arbequina olives and Arbequina olive oil. But the mix is delicious made with bottled Manzanilla olives too.

Makes 250 ml / 8 ¾ fl oz / 1 cup + 1 tablespoon.

30 g / 1 oz / ¼ cup skinned almonds or hazelnuts
150 g / 5 ¼ oz / 1 cup drained, pitted olives
1 spring onion, including some of the green, chopped
2 tablespoons fresh bread crumbs
30 g / 1 oz drained anchovies from a tin
1 tablespoon brandy
Pinch of oregano
Pinch of thyme
Freshly ground black pepper
6 tablespoons extra virgin olive oil
1 tablespoon chopped parsley

Place the nuts in a food processor and process until chopped. Add the olives and onion and process until finely chopped, but not puréed. Transfer to a bowl. Add the crumbs, anchovies, brandy, oregano, thyme, pepper and oil to the processor. Process to make a smooth paste. Stir the paste into the olives. Add the parsley. Serve immediately or refrigerate, tightly covered, up to one week.

Alioli I
GARLIC MAYONNAISE I

Mayonnaise is probably the only classic sauce that is purely Spanish in origin. Legend has it that this famous sauce was invented in Mahón on the island of Menorca. It was supposedly discovered there in 1756 by the Duke of Richelieu, chief of the French invading forces, who either first ate it served by a lowly innkeeper or, possibly, by a saucy Menorcan lady who delighted the duke. He later is said to have popularised the sauce in Paris, calling it *sauce mahonnaise*.

Whatever the origin of the name, mayonnaise is certainly of Spanish or Spanish-Catalan origin. Why? Because mayonnaise is an oil-based sauce and Spain is where olive trees grow. Mayonnaise appears in every tapa bar, from the east to the west, from the south to the north.

In the old days, mayonnaise was hand-made, a leisurely process. Egg yolks are placed in a deep mortar or small bowl. The olive oil, measured into an egg shell, is beaten into the yolks, a few drops at a time until it is slowly incorporated. As the yolks absorb the oil, the sauce magically thickens, emulsifies and expands. The resulting sauce hardly resembles its two basic ingredients at all.

This blender version of traditional mayonnaise uses a whole egg in place of egg yolk. If raw egg could be a health risk, substitute pasteurised egg or make Garlic Mayonnaise II (page 250). For mayonnaise variations, see page 250.

Makes about 240 ml / 8 fl oz / 1 cup

1 to 2 cloves garlic, chopped
1 egg, at room temperature
180 ml / 6 ¼ fl oz / ¾ cup extra virgin olive oil
½ teaspoon salt
3 tablespoons fresh lemon juice or 2 tablespoons vinegar

Put the garlic and egg in a blender and pulse until garlic is finely chopped. With the motor running, pour in the oil in a slow trickle, allowing it to be absorbed by the egg before adding more. Blend in all the oil. The sauce will emulsify and thicken. Blend in the salt and lemon juice.

The sauce will keep, refrigerated, for up to 2 days.

Alioli II
GARLIC MAYONNAISE II

Makes about 240 ml / 8 fl oz / 1 cup.

120 ml / 4 fl oz / ½ cup bottled mayonnaise
4 cloves garlic, crushed
120 ml / 4 fl oz / ½ cup extra virgin olive oil
1 tablespoon lemon juice
Salt

In a bowl, whisk the mayonnaise until smooth. Add the garlic, then beat in the oil. Stir in the lemon juice and add salt to taste.

The sauce will keep, refrigerated, for up to 6 days.

VARIATIONS:

SAFFRON MAYONNAISE
Crush a pinch of saffron threads. Add 2 tablespoons of hot water and allow to steep 10 minutes. Stir the saffron water into the mayonnaise.

QUINCE MAYONNAISE
Stir 45 g / 1 ½ oz quince paste with 2 tablespoons boiling water until softened. Blend into mayonnaise.

HONEY MAYONNAISE
Dissolve 1 tablespoon honey in 2 tablespoons hot water. Stir into the mayonnaise.

RED PEPPER MAYONNAISE
Purée tinned red pimiento and stir it into the mayonnaise

CAPER MAYONNAISE:
Add 3 tablespoons drained capers to the mayonnaise.

Salsa de Pimientos Piquillos
PIQUILLO RED PEPPER SAUCE

This is a sensational dipping sauce or a dressing for vegetables or prawns. And it's ever so simple. The flavour comes from those special peppers, tiny red piquillos from Navarra, that are sweet and piquant at the same time. They are roasted, peeled and packed in tins. All you have to do is open the tin or jar, put the piquillos in a blender with some olive oil. How hard is that? You can add a pinch of thyme or cumin or chopped chilli, if you like it "hot. If you want a warm sauce to serve with hot foods, just heat the sauce gently in a small saucepan.

Makes 200 ml / 7 fl oz.

1 (185-g / 6 ½ -oz) tin piquillo peppers, drained (about 10 peppers)
1 clove garlic
3 tablespoons extra virgin olive oil
1 tablespoon Sherry vinegar
¼ teaspoon salt

Combine the peppers, garlic, oil, vinegar and salt in a blender or food processor. Blend to make a smooth purée. Serve immediately or refrigerate, covered, up to one week.

Salmorejo
GAZPACHO CREAM

This version of gazpacho is famous in the tascas of Córdoba, where it's usually presented in individual ramekins to be eaten with a spoon. It's thick enough to serve as a dip. Serve it in a bowl accompanied by raw vegetables and crisps (chips) as dippers. Salmorejo also becomes a sauce or salad dressing—spoon it over fried aubergine (eggplant) or lettuce hearts. (If you want sipping gazpacho, see the recipe on page 117).

Serves 10 to12 as a party dip or 6 as a starter.

340 g / 12 oz day-old bread, crusts removed
680 g / 1 ½ lb ripe tomatoes, peeled and seeded
3 cloves garlic
5 tablespoons extra virgin olive oil
1 teaspoon salt
1 tablespoon wine vinegar
60 g / 2 oz serrano ham, cut in thin strips, to serve
2 hard-boiled eggs, sliced, to serve

Cut the bread into chunks and put in a bowl with water to cover. Let soak until softened.

Cut the peeled and seeded tomatoes into chunks and place in a food processor bowl with the garlic. Process until puréed.

Squeeze out as much water as possible from the bread. Add the bread to the processor bowl. (If necessary, process in two batches.)

Process until smooth. With the motor running, slowly add the oil, salt and vinegar to make a thick cream. Chill until serving time.

If serving as a dip, spread the cream in a dish and garnish the top with strips of ham and sliced egg. As a starter, serve the cream in individual ramekins or small bowls, each garnished with ham and egg.

Salsa Vinagreta
VINAIGRETTE

This vinaigrette sauce is delicious served with vegetables—asparagus, either fresh or tinned; potatoes, runner beans or *cogollos*, lettuce hearts—or drizzled over grilled fish.

Makes 200 ml / 7 fl oz.

2 hard-boiled eggs
1 clove garlic
¼ teaspoon salt
Freshly ground black pepper
3 tablespoons wine vinegar
120 ml / 4 fl oz / ½ cup extra virgin olive oil
1 spring onion, finely chopped
1 tablespoon chopped parsley

Separate the yolks from the whites. In a blender, combine the egg yolks with the garlic, salt, pepper and vinegar. Blend until smooth. Blend in the oil until it is all incorporated. Stir in the onion and parsley. Chop the egg whites and combine with the sauce. Serve cold or room temperature.

Aliño
SAUCE FOR GRIDDLED FOODS

This simple sauce is spooned over griddled foods immediately before serving. Use it with griddled baby cuttlefish (page 141), griddled chicken breast or any fish fillet. The sauce can also be used as a marinade or basting sauce. Keep it handy when you're cooking meat, poultry or fish on the barbecue.

Makes about 175 ml / 6 fl oz / ⅔ cup.

2 cloves chopped garlic
½ cup chopped parsley
3 tablespoons lemon juice
½ teaspoon salt
Pinch of red chilli flakes (optional)
6 tablespoons extra virgin olive oil

Combine all the ingredients in a small bowl and stir to mix. Use at room temperature. Sauce may be kept, covered and refrigerated, for up to one week.

Mojo Verde
GREEN CHILLI SAUCE WITH CORIANDER

In the Canary Islands, this spicy sauce is served with "wrinkly potatoes," new potatoes that have been boiled in heavily salted water, leaving the skins wrinkled. The sauce is delicious with grilled fish too.

Makes 180 ml / 6 fl oz / ¾ cup.

2 cloves garlic
1 green chilli, such as jalapeño (or to taste)
½ teaspoon ground cumin
1 teaspoon oregano
2 tablespoons chopped parsley
½ cup loosely packed fresh coriander (cilantro) leaves
4 tablespoons olive oil
3 tablespoons wine vinegar
½ teaspoon salt
4 tablespoons water

Place all ingredients in a blender container and blend until smooth. Sauce keeps, covered and refrigerated, one week.

Mojo Colorado
RED CHILLI SAUCE

Serve this as a dipping sauce for tiny new potatoes. It's also good with grilled or steamed fish.

Makes 150 ml / ¼ pint / ⅔ cup.

3 tablespoons pimentón (paprika)
1 fresh red chilli, seeded and chopped, or cayenne to taste
3 cloves garlic
3 tablespoons extra virgin olive oil
3 tablespoons wine vinegar
½ teaspoon ground cumin
½ teaspoon salt
5 tablespoons water

Place all of the ingredients in a blender and blend until smooth. If desired, thin with a little water. Sauce keeps one week, refrigerated.

Y Para Beber

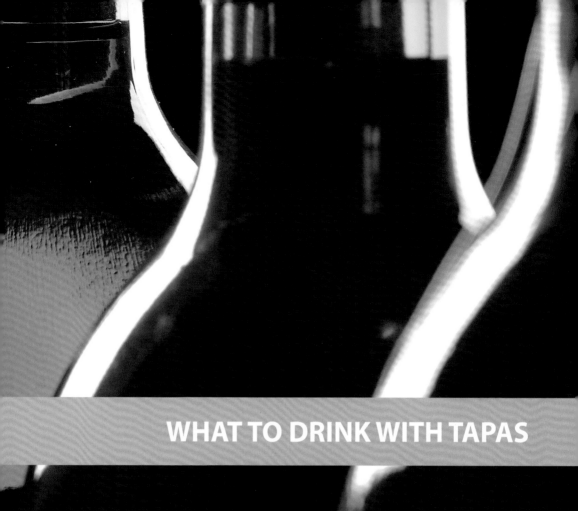

WHAT TO DRINK WITH TAPAS

Y Para Beber
WHAT TO DRINK WITH TAPAS

Selecting Wine

Summertime Red Wine Cooler (*Tinto de Verano*)

Red Wine Sangría (*Sangría*)

Watermelon Sangría (*Sangría de Sandía*)

White Wine Cooler (*Cuerva*)

Sherrytini Cocktail (*Cóctel con Vino de Jerez*)

Sherry-Lemon Cocktail (*Coctel de Jerez con Limón*)

"Valencia Water" (Orange Juice and Cava)
(*Agua de Valencia*)

Cava Cocktail (*Coctel de Cava*)

It's 8 pm on a mild evening and shops and businesses are just closing up. You're on the street, in need of a little refreshment. Catch up with your friends, Pablo, Carmen and Bill. "*¿Una caña?*" How about a beer? You nip into a bar on the plaza and order a round of draught beers, short ones, to wet the throat and whet the appetite. Within minutes people stack up behind you and outstretched hands reach across the bar for glasses of beer and wine, plates of tapas. The beer goes down just fine with a nibble of piping hot ham croquettes.

Maybe Pablo and Carmen head for home, but you and Bill move on to another place, a bodega, or wine cellar, where barrels of wine are stacked. Here, you drink the wine from the barrel which, depending where in Spain you are, might be an oaky red, a dry Sherry, or a mellow Málaga Muscatel. That Muscatel calls for a tabla, board of assorted, sliced sausages. Brilliant pairing.

Many bodegas have real personalities. Some are bullfighting bars, with walls of posters and memorabilia. Others show a flamenco influence and may even have space for a late-night flamenco *tablao*. Some may be where *politicos* gather (subdivided by right-wing and left-wing). Special rooms may be set aside for *tertulias*, round-table chats on subjects from politics to literature, theatre to art. But, the barrels of wine are what a bodega's all about.

Joined by some more friends, you move on to a typical tasca or taberna. Tastes diverge.

Some revert to beer. Others choose white wine and red wine. Someone orders a dry fino Sherry. Another, perhaps the designated driver or a pregnant woman, chooses non-alcoholic beer or *mosto*, not-too-sweet grape juice with no alcohol. With any of these drinks, you can order *raciones*, plates of food to share, or individual tapas.

So, you see, what to drink with tapas depends on what, when, where, with whom. You don't have to stick to a formula, either; you can mix and match to suit yourself.

In general, what you drink with tapas includes beer, cider, fortified aperitif wines such as Sherry and vermouth, cava (sparkling wine), and white, red and rosé wines.

Generally tapas don't go with cocktails or mixed drinks made with stronger spirits (such as gin, whiskey or rum), although these would be appropriate for late-night clubs where you go to dance or to listen to music.

y para beber
WHAT TO DRINK WITH TAPAS

■ SELECTING WINE

Spain has the most extensive vineyards on the planet and is third in the world after France and Italy in volume of wine produced. The numbers are huge, but not just on the quantity scale. Spanish wines are also achieving the highest rankings from leading wine critics. There's a wine for every taste, to match every dish and in every price range. How to choose?

LABEL LINGO. The label on a wine bottle will tell you the name of the wine and the name of the *bodega*, or winery, that produced it. Sometimes the wine's name is the same as the bodega. The label will probably also name a *denominación de origen*, or denomination of origin (DO), which designates the wine's geographic region and is a guarantee of quality. Each DO regulating board establishes requisites for how grapes are cultivated, harvested and turned into wine and for how the wines are to be aged.

The next bit of useful information on the label concerns the grape varietal. You'll see familiar names such as Cabernet Sauvignon, Syrah and Chardonnay, which, although not native varieties, are now widely grown in Spain. The best-known Spanish varietal for red wines is Tempranillo. Often Tempranillo is blended with other varieties, such as Garnacha, Mazuelo and Graciano. The most outstanding white-wine grape is the Albariño, grown in northwest Galicia. Others are Macabeo, Parellada, Airén, Xarel.lo, Viura and Verdejo.

Lastly, a wine label will indicate whether or not a wine has been aged. Most Spanish wine regions classify vintages as *jóven*, young; *crianza*, slightly aged; *reserva*, aged; and *gran reserva*, long aged.

SPANISH WINES—REIGN OF TERROIR

Terroir is a French word meaning "where a wine is coming from"—the sum of soil, climate, grape variety and winemaking style (the word in Spanish, not so well-known, is *terruño*). Not so long ago, you always expected to drink the local wine in your local pub. In a tavern in Sevilla, you sipped Sherry, made in nearby Jerez. In Málaga you drank the local Muscatel. Tascas in Madrid served the easy-drinking wines from nearby La Mancha and Valdepeñas, while Bilbao taverns featured the local white txacolí. Often enough, locally-made wine pairs best with the region's food.

The past 20 years have seen a revolution in how wine is made in Spain, as vintners opt for quality over quantity. Restructuring of vineyards; experimentation with new grape varieties; investment in winery technology, allowing

for controlled fermentation; new oak barrels, and talented wine makers have all contributed to the modernisation trend. The high-alcohol, robust wines quaffed in taverns of old have been replaced by a "new generation" of carefully made wines expressing fresh fruit flavours. Regions once known for their bulk wines are emerging as contenders in the fine wines category.

Here is a guide for tasting your way around Spain. It is by no means a definititive list, for many smaller and lesser-known DO districts are not included here. The wines are grouped by regions. You won't find names of specific wines nor of bodegas (wineries). You'll have to get out there, taste the wines and find your own favourites.

ANDALUSIA Sherry (**Jerez-Xérès-Sherry** and **Manzanilla-Sanlúcar de Barrameda**) is possibly the best known of Spanish wines—going all the way back to Shakespeare's time. The English word, Sherry, is a corruption of the name "Jerez," the town in Andalusia, in the province of Cádiz, where this wine is made. (Jerez is one point of the Sherry triangle that encompasses El Puerto de Santa María and Sanlúcar de Barrameda as well.)

Sherry, made from Palomino grapes, ranges from dry aperitif wines to velvety-smooth dessert wines. It is made by the *solera* method of blending. New wines

are added to the top barrels and, after a proper rest, are introduced into casks of slightly older wine. Fully-matured wine, after several such blendings, is drawn off from the bottom casks. Sherries are fortified wines and have a higher alcoholic content than most table wines (between 15° and 20°).

The dry ones, *fino*, *manzanilla* and *amontillado*, vary in colour from pale straw to topaz. Their flavour is nutty without a trace of sweetness and their aroma is golden. Enjoy them with aperitif foods — olives, nuts, shellfish, cheese, some soups. Mellow, with a hint of sweetness, are the *olorosos* and *palos cortados*, old gold in colour and velvety in texture. These are also appreciated as aperitif wines and pair beautifully with sausage, pâté and blue cheeses. The sweet Sherries are mahogany in colour with a light, never cloying, sweetness, good with nuts as an appetiser, biscuits (cookies) for afternoon tea or with coffee after a meal.

Montilla-Moriles is produced in the province of Córdoba from Pedro Ximénez grapes. Like Sherry, it is made by the *solera* method. Montilla finos are a little edgier than Sherry, with a pleasantly bitter background. They are also considerably less expensive. Like Sherry, they are ideal with most tapas. Amontillado, though produced in Jerez as well, means "made in the style of Montilla." It is more mellow than fino.

The wines of **Málaga** are made primarily from the Pedro Ximénez and Muscatel grapes, both of which produce wines with a high sugar content and a high alcoholic content (as much as 23°). The colour varies from a rich, burnished gold to deepest amber, and the flavour, from sunny fruit to intense raisin. Málaga "dry" goes nicely with tapas, especially sausages and pâtés. The sweet ones are lovely with a selection of pastries or, after dinner, with fresh fruit and cheeses.

ARAGÓN Cariñena wines, dark and solid as ancient castles, high in alcohol, are the perfect accompaniment to the region's lamb and chicken stews. The region's winemaking style is gradually being modernised. **Somontano** is a region in the vanguard of wine-making, with use of "foreign" varietals such as Chardonnay, Cabernet Sauvignon and Gewürztraminer as well as classic Spanish grapes such as Tempranillo. Both reds and whites would be a good choice for a dinner party.

CASTILLA-LA MANCHA La Mancha emcompasses a vast area of vineyards. Wineries range from huge cooperatives to single-estate operations. While there is much experimentation with new grape varieties, red Tempranillo is the star. A lot of investment in this region's wineries is producing new-style, delicious, fruity wines at very affordable prices. **Valdepeñas** is a pocket within the huge La Mancha region. Historically, Valdepeñas wines are those consumed in the tascas of Madrid, so it is a tapas wine, first and foremost. Valdepeñas is a very old wine district that has seen a lot of restructuring. Today it makes impressive Tempranillo reds, great with tapas, especially with Manchego cheese from the same district.

CASTILLA Y LEÓN Ribera del Duero. Arguably, the finest red wines in all of Spain come from this DO, with exceptional wineries making extraordinary wines from Tempranillo, Tinto Fino and Cabernet Sauvignon grapes. (Legendary Vega Sicilia bodegas are in Ribera del Duero.) The style is for powerful, structured wines rather than easy-drinking tapas wines. High ratings mean high prices. **Rueda** is best-known for fruity white wines from the Verdejo grape, while new plantations of Sauvignon Blanc are producing crisp new-style whites. Both are ideal choices with seafood tapas and for light dishes. Verdejo wines are outstanding with many semi-aged cheeses. **Toro** makes classic big wines from Tinta de Toro grapes, but there are modernising trends here. The name, *toro*, translates as "bull." Although it refers to a region around the town of Toro in Zamora province, these wines go well with big, beefy dishes.

CATALONIA The wines of this region are as diverse as the people and the landscape. Though there are some very fine red table wines, the region's climate and varieties seem to favour white wines, which are amongst the finest in Spain. (See also the designation for **CAVA**.) **Penedés** overlaps with cava-producing country. From Penedés come wonderful crisp white wines, light and dry with a delicate perfume, from Xarel.lo, Macabeo and Parellada grapes, good with the region's seafood stews. Juicy reds make this a wine region for all seasons, all tapas. **Priorat.** Old vines in vineyards of low production and visionary wine-making have turned this region into the block-buster of the 21st century. Garnacha and Cariñena are the classic varietals, with Cabernet and Merlot adding interest. These are sumptuous, complex, elegant wines with high prices, probably not for casual tapa-hopping.

GALICIA Galicia occupies the top northwest Atlantic corner of Spain. This is white wine country, but some good reds are produced as well. **Rías Baixas** makes crisp and minerally white wines from the Albariño grape. These are, arguably, Spain's best whites. Vineyards are situated on the banks of *rías*, estuaries, that open out to the Atlantic ocean. Albariño wines are the perfect accompaniment to the tapas of fish and shellfish served in Galicia's taverns.

MURCIA The new-style wines of **Jumilla** concentrate on fresh fruit flavours. Monastrell grapes make for juicy, silky

YOUNG AND FRESH OR WELL-AGED?

In most of Spain's wine regions, red wine vintages are classified as *jóven*, young; *crianza*, slightly aged; *reserva*, aged, and *gran reserva*, long aged. Wines with DO labels must adhere to minimum aging requirements set by their regulating boards. Basically, this means that when you buy a bottle of wine, it's ready to drink. You don't have to cellar it and wait for the tannins to smooth out.

Drink young wines within a year of the time they are made. Good ones are fruity and fresh, with bright cherry or berry colour. Choose youthful wines to drink with tapas, especially with potato tortilla, meatballs, and Spanish sausages such as chorizo. They're perfect with hearty lentil and chickpea stews, with pasta, with paella, with breaded veal cutlet, pork chop, roast chicken. The inexpensive ones are fine for making sangría.

Crianza wines, with just a touch of oak, go well with cheese of all sorts, especially aged Manchego. This is also the perfect wine with most meat dishes, such as grilled steak, roast pork, roast lamb or even a hamburger.

A reserva wine, as the word indicates, means "reserved," a term used in Spanish winemaking to distinguish the finest wines of a vintner's cellar, which are reserved, in bottle, until they are at their optimum for drinking. A reserva wine is made when the grapes in a particular year are of sufficient quality to produce a wine that will improve with aging. These wines, sometimes of a deep, brick colour, are velvety and offer complex bouquet and taste. Choose them to accompany partridge, venison, duck, beef fillet.

reds. Blended with newer varieties, such as Cabernet Sauvignon and Merlot, they produce some outstanding wines. There are some good values from this region, making it a fine choice with tapas.

NAVARRA Contiguous to La Rioja, this region shares many of the characteristics of its neighbour. It is famous for its rosé wines made principally from the Garnacha grape. Sample stylish new red wines made with blends of Tempranillo, Cabernet Sauvignon and Merlot as well as Chardonnay whites. Young wines from Navarra with little or no oak are perfect with a range of tapas.

PAÍS VASCO/EUSKADI (BASQUE COUNTRY) The Basque province of Álava belongs to DO La Rioja. In the provinces bordering the Bay of Biscay, Vizcaya (Bilbao) and Guipúzcoa (San Sebastian), *txacolí*, a zingy, very acidic white wine is produced from the grape varieties Hondarribi Zuri and Hondarribi Beltza. **Txacolí de Getaria, Txacolí de Vizcaya, Txacolí de Alava**. Txacolí is a natural with Basque pintxos, such as salt cod in garlic pil pil sauce.

LA RIOJA This region situated in northern Spain brings together excellent growing conditions with a long, wine-making tradition, resulting in some of Spain's finest table wines, both red and white. It's a region in flux, with old styles co-

existing with newer winemaking trends. Divided into three distinct regions, Rioja Alta, Rioja Baja and Rioja Alavesa, the region produces fairly diverse wines, from the young and fruity to the smooth and oaky. Reds based on the Tempranillo grape, often with the addition of Mazuelo, Graciano and Garnacha, are especially suited for ageing, reaching maturity after several years. Whites are dry and pleasant, predominantly based on the Viura grape. Alongside the classic Rioja style of oak-aged wines are modern wines that express fresh fruit flavours and are only lightly aged on oak. Young Rioja reds are terrific with all manner of tapas. The oak-aged reservas pair beautifully with roast meats and game.

VALENCIA The Comunidad Valenciana comprises the provinces of Alicante, Valencia and Castellón. In the DOs of **Utiel-Requena** and **Valencia**, new winemaking tendencies are showing off the attributes of old varieties such as Bobal and Monastrell. Wines from these regions are huge on the export market. They are good with the region's famous paella and with tapas.

VINO DE PAGO *Pago* means domain, estate or chateau. This is a designation for single-estate wines. So far, there are only a few.

VINO DE LA TIERRA This category was created for wines that don't fit into one of the DOs. They may fall outside of the geographical limitations; be made of varietals not authorized by the regulating boards; produce yields not allowed; or use techniques in growing or vinification not authorized by the denominations. Many of Spain's "new generation" wines have the Vino de la Tierra (VT) label.

CAVA Cava is the Spanish word for sparkling wine made by the *méthode champenoise*, fermented in bottle. (Please don't call it Champagne, because that's a place in France.) Although 99 percent of cavas are produced in Catalonia, the designation is not exclusive to Catalonia. Choose cavas from *brut* and *seco*, gradations of "dry", to *semi-seco*, medium-dry, and *semi-dulce*, medium-sweet. Cava is perfect for celebrations and holiday feasts, but it also makes an elegant match with tapas such as cheese puffs or stuffed mushrooms.

SIDRA DE ASTURIAS Almost no wine is produced in Asturias, where the drink for local imbibing is *sidra*, naturally fermented apple cider. Fizzy, bottled cider can be bought everywhere in Spain, and makes a good summer drink when well chilled.

LIQUORS The word *aguardiente* means any distilled spirit. However, in much of Spain, aguardiente means specifically an anise-flavoured clear brandy, either dry or sweet. In Galicia, *aguardiente de orujo*, is a potent brew that packs the punch of molten lava, literally, "firewater," distilled from the last pressings of grapes. It is a little like French *marc* or Italian *grappa*, clear, dry and with a residual taste of grape. The word *licor* usually means liqueur, a sweetened and flavoured after-dinner drink. Spanish brandy, much of which is produced in Jerez by the makers of Sherry wines, is excellent. It has a rich, mellow taste, but is never as dry as French Cognac. A favourite Spanish digestive is *pacharán*, subtly flavoured with anise and sloe berries. Serve it over ice.

Cuerva
WHITE WINE COOLER

In the bars of Albacete, in eastern La Mancha, this wine drink is mixed in big ceramic bowls and dipped into small cups to serve. The inexpensive white wines of La Mancha are especially suitable for this cooler, but any dry white wine could be used.

Serves 6.

60 g / 2 oz / ⅓ cup sugar
220 ml / 8 fl oz / 1 cup water
Sprigs of fresh mint
1 lemon, sliced
1 orange, sliced
1 bottle dry white wine, chilled
1 apple, chopped
1 peach, chopped
Soda water, if desired
Ice cubes (optional)
Additional mint sprigs for garnish

Combine the sugar and water in a small saucepan. Bring to the boil and cook 5 minutes. Remove from heat and add the mint and half of the lemon and orange slices. Let steep at least 30 minutes.

Strain the sugar syrup into a pitcher or punch bowl and add the wine, remaining lemon and orange slices, apple and peach. Dilute to taste with soda water. Serve small cups or in tall glasses, with ice, if desired. Garnish with mint sprigs.

Tinto de Verano
SUMMERTIME RED WINE COOLER

This is a light and refreshing summer drink, for which there are no set proportions. Keep a bottle of light red wine in the fridge, along with *gaseosa*, bottled, sweetened, fizzy lemonade. Pour wine into a tall glass—with or without ice—add gaseosa to taste. A slice of lemon is good, but not essential.

Sangría
RED WINE SANGRÍA

Sangría makes a great party drink and can be mixed in large quantities. Choose an inexpensive young red wine with no oak. Use any combination of fruit—strawberries, oranges, apples, pears and grapes are some of the best. (Apples float, oranges sink.) Dilute the sangría to taste with fizzy water.

Serves 8 to 10.

60 g / 2 oz / ¼ cup sugar
Strip of orange zest
240 ml / 8 fl oz / 1 cup water
500 ml / 1 pint / 2 cups chopped or sliced fruit
4 tablespoons brandy or liqueur such as Cointreau
1 bottle chilled red wine
500 ml / 1 pint / 2 cups chilled soda water, or to taste

Combine the sugar in a small saucepan with the zest and water. Bring to the boil and simmer 2 minutes. Allow the sugar syrup to cool. Strain it into a pitcher. Discard the orange zest.

Add the fruit and brandy to the pitcher. The fruit can macerate, refrigerated, up to 2 hours. Add the chilled red wine. Immediately before serving, add chilled soda water to taste.

Serve the sangría and fruit in glasses or goblets.

Sangría de Sandía
WATERMELON SANGRÍA

Prepare this colourful wine punch in advance and chill it. Or, if preferred, mix it and serve immediately over ice cubes.

Serves 8.

3 tablespoons sugar
Strip of orange zest
120 ml / 4 fl oz / ½ cup water
900 g / 2 lbs ripe watermelon
3 tablespoons Cointreau or Triple Sec
1 bottle dry white wine, well chilled
A few strawberries
Sprigs of mint

Place the sugar and zest in a saucepan with the water. Bring to the boil and stir to dissolve the sugar. Remove from the heat and cool. Discard the orange zest.

Remove seeds and green rind from the watermelon. Save a few chunks of flesh for garnish. Puree the flesh in a blender or food processor. Sieve the puree and place in a pitcher with the sugar syrup, Cointreau or Triple Sec, and white wine. Chill the sangría for 1 hour.

Serve the sangría, over ice if desired, garnished with the reserved cubes of watermelon, whole strawberries, and mint sprigs.

Cóctel con Vino de Jerez
SHERRYTINI COCKTAIL

Dry Sherry stands in for vermouth in this twist on a classic cocktail. If you use manzanilla Sherry, spike the drinks with Manzanilla olives. If you choose dry fino, finish with a twist of orange peel. Warming the twist over a lighted match releases the citrus fragrance. Chill the martini glasses before mixing the cocktail.

Makes 4 cocktails.

8 olives or 4 twists orange peel
Cracked ice
240 ml / 8 fl oz gin
60 ml / 2 fl oz manzanilla or fino Sherry

Stick olives on 4 cocktail sticks and place in four chilled martini cocktail glasses. Or, if using orange peel, hold each strip of peel, skin side down, briefly over a lighted match. Drop the orange peels into cocktail glasses.

Place ice in a jar or cocktail shaker. Add the gin and Sherry. Shake or stir. Strain the Sherrytini into the cocktail glasses and serve.

Coctel de Jerez con Limón
SHERRY-LEMON COCKTAIL

Grenadine is pomegranate syrup. It gives a fruity flavour and a deep blush to this cocktail. If available, add a few ruby seeds from a fresh pomegranate to the drink. Brandy de Jerez is Spanish brandy from the same region where Sherry is made.

Makes 4 cocktails.

Cracked ice
120 ml / 4 fl oz dry Sherry
120 ml / 4 fl oz Brandy de Jerez
6 tablespoons grenadine syrup
4 tablespoons lemon juice
4 strips lemon peel

Put the ice in a cocktail shaker. Pour over the Sherry, brandy, grenadine and lemon juice. Shake the cocktail. Strain into four cocktail glasses. Hold each twist of lemon peel, skin side down, briefly over a lighted match and drop it into the cocktail.

Agua de Valencia
"VALENCIA WATER" (ORANGE JUICE AND CAVA)

Valencia is famed for its orange groves. Fresh juice plus bubbly cava makes a great festive drink.

Serves 6.

570 ml / 1 pint / 2 ⅓ cups fresh orange juice (from 7 to 8 oranges)
75 ml / 3 fl oz / ⅓ cup orange-flavoured liqueur, such as Triple Sec or Cointreau
75 ml / 3 fl oz / ⅓ cup light rum or gin
½ bottle chilled *semi-seco* (medium-dry) cava
Ice (optional)

Combine the orange juice in a pitcher with the liqueur and rum. Immediately before serving, add the cava. Add ice, if desired. Serve immediately in goblets or wine glasses.

Coctel de Cava
CAVA COCKTAIL

Bubbly with a festive flair. Grenadine is a sweet syrup made from pomegranate juice.

Makes 6 cocktails.

4 tablespoons grenadine
1 bottle chilled *brut* (extra dry) cava
Pomegranate seeds (optional)

Place 2 teaspoons grenadine in each of six flute glasses. Fill with chilled cava. Add a few pomegranate seeds to each, if desired. Serve immediately.

GLOSSARY

Aceite de oliva virgen extra: Extra virgin olive oil.

Aceituna: Olive.

Adobo: Marinade with vinegar and herbs for uncooked fish or meat.

Albóndiga: Meatball.

Aliño: Sauce, salad dressing.

Alioli: Garlic mayonnaise.

Bacalao: Cod, usually salt cod.

Barril: Barrel, wine butt, beer keg.

Bellota: Acorn. Designates ham from ibérico pigs fattened on acorns.

Bocadillo: Sandwich.

Bodega: Cellar, winery, bar with wine barrels.

Bollo: Bread roll, bun.

Boquerón: Fresh anchovy.

Buñuelo: Fritter.

Caldo: Broth, stock, consommé.

Callos: Tripe.

Caña: Draught beer.

Cava: Spanish sparkling wine made by the *méthode champenoise*.

Cazuela, cazuelita: Earthenware casserole, small pottery ramekin; food cooked in a casserole.

Cecina: Salt-cured beef or venison.

Cerveza: Beer.

Chorizo: Dry-cured sausage, usually pork, flavoured with garlic and pimentón (paprika).

Cocido: One-pot meal containing, meat, chicken, legumes and vegetables.

Denominación de origen. DO: Denomination of origin, used for wines and foods regulated by geographic origin and quality controls.

Embutidos: Sausages.

Empanada, empanadilla: Savoury pie, small pie or pasty.

Escabeche: Marinade with vinegar for cooked fish, meat, game or vegetables. **En escabeche:** pickled.

Freiduría: Shop where fried foods, usually seafood, are prepared and sold.

Gamba: Prawn, shrimp.

Garbanzo: Chickpea.

Gazpacho: Andalusian cold soup, usually with tomatoes, but also with almonds.

Guindilla: Hot chilli, pickled green chilli.

Ibérico: Iberian; a breed of pig used for ibérico ham.

Jamón ibérico: Cured ham made from ibérico breed pigs in south-western Andalusia, Extremadura and western Castilla.

Jamón serrano: Cured ham made anywhere in Spain from cross-breed pigs, such as Duroc, Large White.

Jerez: Sherry wine.

Langostino: Large prawn (shrimp).

Marisco: Shellfish.

Mojama: Salt-cured tuna.

Morcilla: Blood sausage, black pudding.

Paella: Rice cooked with other ingredients in a wide, flat pan.

Paleta: Shoulder, front leg of a pig, cured as for ham.

Pil pil: A garlic and olive oil sauce, usually with salt cod.

Pimentón: spice made from dried sweet red peppers; paprika. **Pimentón dulce:** sweet pimentón; **pimentón agridulce:** bittersweet pimentón; **pimentón fuerte:** hot pimentón, but not as hot as cayenne.

Pimentón de la Vera: Smoke-dried pimentón produced in La Vera (Extremadura).

Pimiento: Pepper (vegetable), red or green capsicum, fresh or roasted.

Piquillo: Small red sweet pepper, usually tinned.

Plancha: Griddle (American, grill pan) for cooking on a hob (stovetop).

Pringá: Leftover cooked fat pork, meat and sausages chopped up and spread on bread.

Queso: Cheese.

Ración: Plateful, serving (larger than a tapa).

Recebo: Designates ham from pigs finished on pig feed and grain, rather than acorns.

Reserva: Aged wine.

Serrano: Mountain. Also, type of salt-cured ham.

Sidra: Apple cider.

Taberna: Tavern, bar, pub.

Tasca: Tavern, bar, pub.

Tomate frito: Tomato sauce, usually pureed. Also, tinned tomato sauce.

Tortilla: Eggs cooked in a round, flat disk with other ingredients, usually potatoes.